Don't Fail at Failure

By
Stuart Humber

Copyright © 3P Publishing
First published in 2021 in the UK

3P Publishing
C E C, London Road Corby
NN17 5EU

A catalogue number for this book is available from the
British Library

ISBN: 978-1-913740-28-3

Cover design: James Mossop
Author Photography: Krystal Clear

Contents

Introduction

They say everyone has a book within them; I have been trying to write mine for years. Numerous times I have woken up on a Sunday morning with the ambition of making it happen; written the first few thousand words, only to read it weeks later and feel dissatisfied and disappointed. Every time I would pencil in a few words it became a diary of my achievements and failings with no real focus or direction. I didn't know what I was really writing about or who the book was written for. If I was to spend a large amount of my time seated with a laptop in front of me, neglecting my loved ones and procrastinating on my daily duties around the family home, then I would want to know it was for something; not something that just satisfied my ego, but something others could learn from and relate to.

Although this is still mostly a book about my ultra-athletic failures and later successes, it isn't necessarily a book for ultra-distance hobbyists. This is directed to anyone who fears failure or discomfort and automatically shies away from the hardship. Everyone fails and everyone feels pain. The biggest lesson in life is not to fear it; it's inevitable and you will spend many days, weeks, months and years on the roller coaster of joy and pain. It's your choice how you ride it. Will you hold on tight and roll with it; riding the roller coaster for all its worth to see where the next destination is; or will you plant your heels in the ground, tense up, and stubbornly fight against its inevitable progress. I promise these are two totally different journeys.

The first full of education, growth, progression and fulfilment, and the other will come with a sense of feeling dissatisfied, angry, frustrated, jealous and ultimately regretful.

Once I stopped fighting against the inevitable and relaxed into the ups and downs of life, I began using the downs as a platform to grow and learn from, which made the ups ever more joyful and satisfying. There are no bigger teachers than failure and pain. Coming from failure after failure and experiencing the pain, both emotionally and physically, encouraged me to adapt, to learn, and to find a new path which wasn't necessarily pain-free, but to a place where I was in control of the pain, choosing how and when I would feel it. I even looked for failure. This helped with understanding where my limits were. The fascinating thing was that my mental and physical pain thresholds grew exponentially: every time I was broken, the point at which I failed increased.

An amazing life-changing progress happened during the last few years, and it wasn't to me, it was my wife, Teri. Teri's life went from living with physical disability, depression, anxiety, sorrow and daily pain, which sent her into complete shutdown and an unwillingness to fight for anything better, to a life without the disability: a life full of adventure, growth, changes, challenges, lessons and fulfilment. Both lives came with their own pains and discomforts; the only change was, we stopped failing at them, and started using them as our education, and an opportunity.

I hope you get at least one gem from my book. That's all I look for in any book. If there's just one sentence, one paragraph or one lesson in any book I've read or listened to, that resonated with me, then I didn't waste my time. It's those little golden nuggets that make you stare at the wall in deep thought. It's those diamonds that can be hidden between the lines and behind the words that can change your journey. My ambition is to make you stare out of the window in contemplation just once.

Thank you and enjoy.

Part 1
The Journey So Far

Chapter 1
Eagle Plains

As my eyes open for the umpteenth time after a very restless and nervous night on the 13th of March 2013, it takes a few moments to register where I am and what the next few hours and days require of me. Eagle Plains is the location, 10.30am is the time, and the 6633 Arctic Ultra is the name of the game!

Eagle Plains is a very remote truck stop sitting in the middle of the Yukon in Canada. Its nearest neighbour is Fort McPherson, 182 kms north-east along the Dempster Highway. It's a small community of around 700 that became established because of the Hudson's Bay Company settling there over 50 years ago, selling fur around the world. Drive in the opposite direction from Eagle Plains for 404 kms and you will reach Dawson City, an historic town in Canada because of the Klondike gold rush between 1896 and 1899. Over 100,000 prospectors flooded the region in search of riches and a new life. The population currently stands at around 1375, making it the second biggest town in the Yukon, with plenty of prospectors still looking for their big find. As you can see, overpopulation isn't one of the region's problems, and this becomes very apparent at Eagle Plains.

The truck stop is pretty much what you would expect from a secluded truck stop, hundreds of miles from anywhere, in the middle of the frozen Canadian wilderness. It's a single storey, extra-large wooden hut, with a small sign on the roof, holding both the Canadian and Yukon flags, which were frozen in time from the Arctic conditions. In fact, a few horses secured to a wooden log by their reins outside the entrance wouldn't go amiss.

Inside feels like a hunter's lodge with a few stuffed animals scattered randomly around the reception and within the bar area. A long corridor running away from the reception area to the right is where all the single and double rooms are located; nearly all are currently occupied by the other 27 participants and organisers of this ludicrous race: a race known for being the toughest, coldest and windiest ultra-distance foot race on the planet called the 6633 Arctic Ultra.

After a minute or two, I am able to focus my already tired eyes and notice Mark Fuscard is still lucky enough to be catching a few ZZZs. Mark was my roommate for the few nights that we spent in accommodation before and after the race. He is a very generous, helpful and welcoming roommate, slightly older than me with skin that looks like he loved the outdoors, and a mannerism that made me feel like this wasn't his first rodeo. He lives in a small village off the coast of Cornwall, in the South West of England, enjoying what came across as a perfect work/life balance existence with his long-term partner. He spent his working days in the Coastguard as an air ambulance paramedic, which was also the charity he was raising money for by taking part in this event, and his leisure time making the most of nature's playground. Along with all the others, Mark made me feel a little inadequate, a child in an adults' world. He looked very much in control of the situation, full of confidence about his ability and very methodical in his organisation. From the moment I left my wife, Teri, and two daughters, Myia and Keira, five days earlier at Heathrow airport in London, I had felt out of place, out of my comfort zone and totally underprepared for this mammoth challenge.

As my world drove out of the drop-off zone at the airport, the overwhelming feeling of loneliness passed over me. I had never been very accepting of my own company; I become quite anxious when I'm on my own, away from home. This was magnified as I spent the first 13 years of my relationship with Teri as her part-time carer because of the disabilities she suffered from, creating a shadow over us. (This will be explored more fully in chapter 2.)

The first leg of the three-flight journey to Whitehorse was to Chicago with a very brief 1 hour 10 minute transfer; and for anyone that has been through O'Hare International Airport, you know you can't get from one end to the other within an hour without testing your legs. Next stop was Vancouver for a not-so-quick stopover. It was around ten hours between the flights, and to add to the displeasure, the ten hours was through the night. With so many other preparations I was negotiating for my little adventure, I had overlooked this. If I had been better organised, I would have booked a room for the night, but as it was, I was forced to spend the night in the airport, which surprisingly closed for the evening and wasn't opening again until 6am. All shops, cafes, food venues and customer services were closed. All staff and customers disappeared for the night, and all travellators and escalators had been switched off. This is not helpful when you're dragging around two suitcases and hand luggage looking for sustenance and hydration.

I walked along every corridor, poked my head around every unlocked doorway, investigated every hall and peered through every window, trying to find some nutrition and somewhere to place my head for a few hours. The only companions I had throughout the whole airport was a solitary cleaner, who I think was Mexican and quite shy, and a free-spirited hippy from the Czech Republic with enough of the magic green leaves inside him to make sure he was out for the count for most of the night. I did feel for him around four o'clock when he woke up with the munchies, and all I had to offer him was a breakfast bar from my event food stash. Six o'clock eventually came and the world woke up. After throwing some food and coffee down, I found my way to the small 30-ish seater jet that lifted its wheels as the day broke, landing two hours later in Whitehorse.

Martin Likey, the director of the race, was there to greet me and drove me along with a couple of others to the hotel where further racers and crew were staying. Still feeling very anxious about being away from my world, I was thrown into a new world, full of ultra-athletes, all of them far more experienced, knowledgeable, equipped and better dressed than this little mouse I was staring at in the mirror of my hotel bedroom. What the bloody hell was I doing, I whispered to myself as Mark walked into the room and introduced himself. I'm not sure if he noticed the panic that was brewing inside me, but chatting with him, settled my stress down. I took the opportunity to join him that afternoon for a stroll around the town and to grab some expedition food packs, and last-minute, not-so-essential, essential items. A bit of retail therapy always helps! Fond memories remain from those two nights at Whitehorse as I spent many an hour sat in the comfy seats of the bar, witnessing how meticulous the other racers were with their equipment and how they would explain, with great pride, to anyone who was within ear shot, the decision to buy a specific stove or a particular jacket or brand of footwear. I loved listening from the side-lines to everyone's stories as they came and went in small groups to grab a coffee or a pint. The gatherings always resembled the scene from the film 'Jaws' when Robert Shaw, Roy Schieder and Richard Dreyfuss compared war wounds just before the great white showed them how small they really were. Similarly, these last few days were just before Mother Nature was about to show us how insignificant we really are.

The next day came with the event briefing to clarify a few things, and a two hour event trial run around a local lake. Basically, this was to make sure everything was working, we were competent enough to look after ourselves and were capable of cooking food. This was also the last day for any essential and not-so-essential shopping.

On the morning of the 11th, we were all packed into a convoy of hefty 4x4s for the long drive to Eagle Plains, via a night stop-over at Dawson City to split the 580-mile journey. We slept at the Downtown Hotel, which is infamous for the one and only Sourtoe Cocktail drink. This is a simple cocktail consisting of a shot of whiskey liquor garnished with a frostbitten human toe, obviously not still attached. The story goes as follows: In the 1920s, there lived a couple of brothers called the Linkin brothers - Louie and Otto - who ran rum. One day they got caught out in a horrendous blizzard straying them off the road, which led to Louie misplacing his footing as he slipped through a patch of ice, soaking his foot. When the brothers got back to their cabin, Louie's right foot was frozen solid. Otto axed off his brother's toe, preventing gangrene setting in, and placed it into a jar of alcohol to commemorate the event. As legend has it, in 1973, Captain Dick Stevenson found the jar (and the toe) in a remote cabin and came up with the idea of the Sourtoe Cocktail Club — an exclusive club with one membership requirement: to gain admittance to the club, potential members must drink the legendary Sourtoe Cocktail. There's just one rule: "You can drink it fast. You can drink it slow. But your lips must touch that gnarly toe."

So, challenge set, and challenge accepted. One by one, every one of our party proceeded to knock back a smooth local whiskey liquor with what looked like an aged black squidgy toe in it, allowing it to touch their lips. I was the last one of the night to enjoy the unique cocktail so, waiting in the background, I tried to get a sneaky look at what must be a lifelike sausage replica of a human toe.

After all, it couldn't possibly be a real human toe, could it? My time came, and as I sat on the special seat, I managed to get a good close look at what was, undoubtedly, a real human toe. Where would they get a real human toe from? This surpasses any drinking game I've had the pleasure to partake in during my cloudy years. Apparently, they are all donated. This specific toe I was about to kiss on the first date was the eighth edition, coming from an anonymous donor. The donation had been sent in a jar of alcohol with a piece of paper, penned on with a warning, "Don't wear open-toed sandals when mowing the lawn". With 30 onlookers waiting for me to become better acquainted with my drink, I sat nervously. "Come on Stu, KISS IT, KISS IT", I heard, so a second later I could feel the whiskey warm my throat as it trickled down, then instantly realised the toe had gone into my mouth. Before heaving, and definitely before swallowing it, as that would encompass a $2500 fine and being labelled as cannibalism, I spat it back into the glass. On a positive note, the whiskey contributed to a good night's sleep.

Waking up confused, and before adjusting to my environment in the compact room of the Downtown Hotel, I sat up and stared through the murky glass into Dawson City for the first time. It was dark when we had arrived the evening before, so I wasn't fully aware of my surroundings. Dawson City looks to accommodate about five hundred dwellings, set up in the traditional fashion of block after block. My room was on the top floor so I could comfortably see a large percentage of its geography. Apart from the hotel we were staying in, I couldn't see any other life; it was a ghost town. A white, eerie, motionless ghost town. Hopefully, we have time to explore, I thought. I was told we had an hour or so before the wheels would start moving again to take us up the road to the start line. Their concept of 'up the road' is a little different from mine. 250 miles in England isn't just up the road, it's across the country or even going on holiday, but in Canada, it is, according to them, just up the road.

Strolling around the neglected, weather-beaten streets, there was no sound apart from the comforting crunch of the fresh, thin, virgin layer of snow. Once again, I was taken to a place that I believed only existed in the TV world, maybe an abandoned country and western set, left and forgotten in time. The solitude didn't last long as the silence was broken by a shout a few streets away. Martin was calling in the troops; it was time. We piled back into the 4x4s and the convoy was heading up the road once again. This time the atmosphere was heavier as we sat scrunched together for another six hours. The butterflies were making their presence known as they started fluttering in my stomach, so I'm guessing, if everyone felt the same, the anxiousness was squeezing the chest of us all, and the stories that were so prevalent the previous day, subsided.

Scarcely a word was said all day and into the evening. Arriving at our destination as the daylight was fading, we were all allocated our dormitories for the night, retrieved our sleds, grabbed a quick bite from the restaurant and disappeared to our rooms. Isolated in our little worlds, the final preparations unfolded. Firstly, sleds were built, then drop bags filled. Clothing placed neatly beside each bed ready to jump into the next day. Sleeping bags, bivvies and sleeping mats all constructed together for easy roll-out to save time later. Everything perfectly placed in position within the sleds to create the best balance, and any last hygiene issues taken care of. I've grown to love this feeling of the pre-race prep; you can feel the heart beating more deeply, blood feels like lava as it reaches every cell, and the roller coaster of contentment mixed with anticipation and eagerness fuels your senses. The evening turned to night, and when as much as could be done, had been done, it was back to staring at the ceiling until the eyelids met in the middle.

It's 9.30am; I'm standing outside the truck stop staring down the Dempster highway that rolls away into the furthest skyline I've ever seen, and this vastness in front of me is but a fraction of the journey that lay ahead. I'm already feeling nostalgic as I stand on the start line, with only one hour left until the gun fires, and 27 new-age adventurers take a step forward to change their perspective of what is possible and to find their limits physically, mentally and spiritually. This moment has a very eerie and surreal feel to it, as if Stephen King wrote it himself. Participants are checking, double-checking then doing it all again; changing their layers and then changing back, repeatedly paying visits to the toilet to relieve pre-race nerves. Organisers are loading vehicles, checking weather, whispering directions and duties into each other's ears. It's currently -26 degrees C with an almost unnoticeable breeze. There are a couple of frost-crusted trucks parked up on the right of the building, and the sun is trying to make an appearance at the end of a vast landscape, creating a spectrum of colours I have never seen before. From the start line looking in at this colony of misfits which, to be honest, we must be to even attempt something so ridiculous as this, watching them scurry around like a bunch of worker ants, my mind starts to wander. I start thinking, WHY? Why was I here? Why did I leave 'my world' at the airport? Why did I think I was competent enough to finish this event? What chain of events had happened to lead to this? Could I really get through another challenge relying on ego and stubbornness? Had I bitten off more than I could chew this time? I had no answers and no more time to think; this was it, I was here, and I had 30 minutes until it was game time. I still needed one more visit to the toilet, one more change of clothing, grab a few more calories and place my sled at the start.

Counting down 10-9-8-7, 20 to 30 yards in front of me was Martin with a gun in his hand pointing towards the heavens. It was like watching a movie with the sound off as I couldn't hear anything - complete silence - my stress hormones had reached such level that I guess the need to hear wasn't so important. 6...5...4... he continued as I stared at his mouth trying to see his lips mime the words...3...2...1, through his frozen, misty breath...BANG.

Chapter 2
My World

I feel that, in order for you to understand how much of a transformation it was for me to become successful at failure, I need you to understand where I've come from and how certain characteristics came to be embedded in me. I believe it is important to understand your own past so you can free yourself from it and develop your future.

I currently live in Lutterworth, a small town in the south of Leicestershire, slap bang in the middle of England, with my amazing wife Teri and two beautiful daughters, Myia and Keira. I spent my educational years in Lutterworth attending the local High School and College. School for me was torturous; I hated it. I hated the routine, I hated the discipline, I hated the pack mentality; I just hated being around so many people. It was so difficult to be the grey person; so hard to be on my own and find solitude. I longed to stick my head in the sand, not raising it again until eleven more years had passed so I could escape. I was very shy, never academic, and felt uneasy being so far away from my safe places.

My parents divorced when I was six years old after grinding their way through years of being in such an unhappy relationship, which regularly ended in fighting. Throwing pots against the walls, slamming doors with raised voices became just a regular weekend occurrence. I think this is where my need to hide, to disappear and to become invisible, came from. When the tension grew and the angry voices reverberated off the walls, I would hide underneath our small square dining table behind the overly large tablecloth in the centre of the dining room.

This was my first-ever safe place. This is where, if I really, really concentrated, I was able to levitate. I would close my eyes so tight, disengaging from the present, imagining leaving this room, leaving this town, leaving this city and this country. I would fantasise about flying higher and higher, further and further from anything that was hurting me. I would reach all the beauty this planet has to offer and the magnificent wonders of the world. I would hurtle past the pyramids, circle the Eiffel Tower, swoop into the Grand Canyon and chase all the wildlife along the Serengeti. I wouldn't return until the volume in the house had decreased or a slammed door snapped me back to my safe place under the table.

After my parents divorced, my mum tried her best to look after the three of us. I am the eldest of three siblings, with a brother and a sister. Raising three young children at that time, as a single parent, was extremely difficult. The financial deficit became too much of a burden to cope with for my mum, even with two jobs. It wasn't long before the three of us needed to move in with our dad and his new wife, who came with her own ready-made family. Three children became five, instantly giving me a new stepbrother and a stepsister. I was the new kid on the block, very shy, vulnerable, and lacking in self-belief. The bottom of the pecking order belonged to me. I didn't know how to behave or contribute within an already-established pack of up-and-coming alpha males, so with this, my ranking in the group rapidly became apparent. I was to be the fall guy and the one to blame if things went wrong. Constantly being pecked at, although not enough to create attention, but enough to keep me in the position of the swab on the ship.

My bedroom became my next safe place, even though I did share the room with my new stepbrother, Ross. This wasn't too big of an issue because, luckily, he was never there. Ross bettered me in everything: sports, school, confidence and friends. Being the same age, all my initial so-called friends were his friends first. We played for the same football team where he was the man of the match and I was the substitute. We were in the same year at school and took some of the same classes, which actually benefited me on occasion. When the other students realised, I was Ross's stepbrother, they regarded me as someone a little higher in the hierarchy. We went to the same Cub Scout group, another activity I bloody hated because of the attention and the team activities. It's not a nice feeling to be the last one picked in everything. As much as Ross progressed, I lost confidence and became further withdrawn. I couldn't, and didn't, hold it against him. It wasn't his fault. I honestly thought of him as a brother, respecting him for his achievements and hoping he would further improve. The bit that hurt the most was that my dad became his dad, and Ross's achievements, especially sporting achievements, overshadowed my sporting incompetence. You see, my dad could have been a professional footballer if certain circumstances had gone his way. He held the same dominance of character and hierarchical ranking as Ross in our village. Everyone knew him and wanted to be around him, so I guess he saw a bit of himself in Ross. I felt an embarrassment because of my inadequacies, especially living under the label of Richard's son. Certain expectations came with the honourable title of Richard's son - I didn't fulfil them, but Ross did.

It was just before my 13th birthday when I made a decision; a decision I had been considering for quite a few months, if not, years. I decided to run away from the discomfort of my life with my dad. The habit which had slowly grown from the very first need to escape, run and hide under that dining room table, and it became easier and easier. Whenever I felt in an uncomfortable situation, I would become Houdini, using any technique I could to evade, avoid or disappear. The next day on the journey to school I pleaded with the bus driver to pull over, as I was feeling unwell. I departed the school bus and jumped onto the next public bus travelling in the opposite direction towards the city, where I would join my mum and start a new life. Even though I had considered it for a while, that day wasn't planned. I woke up one morning with the need to escape. There were now six children in the house, with the birth of Jonathan. Jonathan, a sweet-natured and loving baby brother, was born with a mild case of autism, or something similar, as the subject was never discussed. Space was becoming scarce in our four-bedroom end terrace with four of us quickly becoming teenagers. It was obvious we all needed our own space. With teenage hormones banging off the walls, tension and arguments were frequent, hiding in corners became near impossible. So, I ran to the city, with my sister and brother following my lead within the year. I didn't see my dad again for five years. All in all, I've only seen him a handful of times since, with the last words spoken between us over ten years ago.

I had three years left before my final exams. The journey to school consisted of two buses, a two-mile walk to catch the first and a further mile walk to catch a second. This allowed me to create lots of imaginative situations and scenarios along the way, which hopefully meant I couldn't make it to school. My attendance for the last few years hovered around fifty percent. Not the best for my exams, but the usual habits continued. School was too uncomfortable, so I didn't go. I finished my education with only two lower-level qualifications - Maths and Woodwork.

Adulthood beckoned. I finished school with pretty much bugger all, but I was over the moon. I can't recall any pleasant memories from my first 16 years, so I blocked them out and moved positively forward, looking ahead for a fresh start where nobody knew me or my past self-loathing. I floated through the next ten years or so with a couple of steady relationships, one of them developing into my first short, failed marriage. Truth be told, the foundation of the marriage was built on both of us coming from previous relationships and looking for a replacement; a rebound relationship. I spent most days working twelve to fourteen hours and we grew apart, ending the marriage amicably.

I tried whatever roles of employment fell into my lap. I started straight out of school training to be a truck mechanic, but pulled out six months before receiving qualifications, because this was unfortunately in the middle of the recession of the early 90s and there was no work. I then spent six months being a baker, and then a delivery guy delivering greeting cards. My best and most successful career was as a printer. I accumulated six years of experience with a rapidly growing greeting card printing company, eventually fulfilling an impressive workshop manager role by the age of 22. This confidence in my ability within the field led me to two unsuccessful attempts at owning my own printing businesses. The first attempt was a partnership that collapsed because, although I knew a lot about printing, I knew nothing about business. I made a few bad judgement calls, placing my trust in the wrong people, and the company was forced to close. Left with loyal customers and a newly acquired tough lesson in business, I tried again.

But once again, it was goodnight sweetheart as the printing world took a big hit with the technological advancements in computers and digital printers. My skill set in printing died and I once again grabbed whatever job opportunity came along. I spent the next six to seven years jumping from one position to another at an ASDA distribution centre, starting as a warehouse colleague, then trainer, team leader, and eventually a truck driver. I finished with a year as an assistant merchandiser in the clothing retail department of George at ASDA.

It was my 27th year before I actually fought for anything, breaking the usual habit of fleeing once things turned hard. This was my relationship with Teri. We became an item at the beginning of 2001, moving in with each other two days into the relationship. To this day I don't know how, and why, it progressed into a full-on relationship. I wasn't exactly a catch. I was homeless, living in my Ford XR3i, and I had been drunk for the previous six months. After getting a divorce from my first marriage, losing my printing business, and being declared bankrupt in the same month, I decided to go for a drink. This disturbing month led the way to drink, drugs, gambling and partying, and lasted for six months. Every day was the same. I could be found either drinking and partying, working, or grabbing a couple of hours sleep or unconsciousness, whatever label you care to give it with so much alcohol consuming me. This then progressed into the lowest point of my life, 48 hours before my relationship with Teri started. I attempted suicide on New Year's Eve 2000 with a crate of beer and a fist full of tablets. The intention was to build enough Dutch courage to consume the tablets. Luckily, I passed out from the alcohol before I could put the tablets into my mouth. The next morning, I remember waking up to witness a scene from the film Trainspotting. Empty beer cans all over the bed, tablets scattered as if someone filled a pill pinata from a chemist and smashed it open above the bed. I had vomited onto the pillow next to me, and urinated. I didn't bother trying to clean the mess up; rather I wrapped up the whole sorry mess up in the bed sheet and threw it in the bin along with my emotional connection to it.

I know, I hear you, what a catch I hear you say, but 48 hours later I'm living with Teri. WOW, how does that happen?

From day one of the relationship Teri had her own baggage, too. She had recently finished a shitty marriage, which brought with it some deep trust issues. Along with her physical and mental health problems, our first seven to eight years were very unpleasant and painful but brought with them life lessons that would greatly benefit our time together further along our journey. It was, in these first few years, however, that the most amazing thing happened to me; I became a dad. Me, a dad. I barely knew how to be a Stuart. But it was the most amazing feeling, instantly becoming the most important role in my life.

Teri's health started deteriorating a couple of years before I arrived in the picture. Her days would vary drastically; one day being able-bodied, fully capable of maintaining an active, contributing life, and looking very normal to the outside world. The consequences of a normally active day would lead to the next day being full of pain, weakness and an unresolvable overall body ache. There would be days where she'd be unable to take care of her own hygiene, or to do the easiest of household tasks to make her feel like she was contributing to the partnership and the welfare of our family. I accepted this from the very beginning during our first conversations, with the understanding that if we were to take this relationship further, she would need patience, empathy, encouragement and support. With my naivety and my longing to be the hero, I explained I would be there to help and support her in whatever the future threw at us. I would be everything she needed me to be.

As I have already mentioned, the next seven years were tough, developing into one of the most important learning curves in my life. It's fair to say I wasn't particularly good at living up to my promise I had made to Teri at the beginning. Juggling work, housekeeping, caring for Teri, caring for the girls, and trying to maintain who I was, became overwhelming and something had to give. Unfortunately, keeping what I perceived to be Stuart high on my priority list, i.e., drinking, gambling, smoking, motorbikes, cars, etc, created constant tension in camp: disappointment and anger on Teri's part, and resentment on mine. Some very heated arguments followed, and on a multitude of occasions resulted in me being kicked out of the house. Seven years of going around in circles, and me turning everything around in my favour led to a massive fallout and separation. This, as it turned out, was the best thing that happened to us. It slapped me in the face and made me realise it was time I changed. This very harsh reality check showed me that my needs weren't the most important anymore. There were now three people in my world that ranked higher on the list than me.

Teri's condition continued to get worse. What was once an arm and shoulder issue slowly progressed to her lower body, and walking started to become difficult. My workload had not changed. I was still working full-time, in fact, more than full-time. I was throwing in at least 50-hour weeks as a truck driver and I was still doing the best I could to cover Teri's needs, looking after the girls, taking care of the house duties, cooking, cleaning, ironing, shopping, paying the bills, etc. But now things were different, now I was in control. Nothing else had really changed except me. I had learnt to hide my needs; I was learning how to be empathetic, I was learning how to listen, and I was forgetting what made me, me. My life became regimented, even military. I knew what I had planned for every single second of every single day. This made me very dominating when it came to family decision-making, such as where we spent money, where we had days out or even what we should have for dinner. I switched off, becoming very controlling. I didn't feel happiness, sadness, anger, or excitement. I had no emotional connection to any event or situation.

Everything was just another task that needed overcoming and I would treat it as such. Even the fun stuff like Christmas, birthdays or holidays became a job, a chore that simply got added to my list. I still believe to this day it was a necessary consequence for us, as a family, to survive the life we were all stuck in. Short term, it's manageable and repairable if you find yourself being forced to overcome a difficult situation, but for the long haul, it can breed a very unhappy and unhealthy environment. It doesn't matter how much you convince yourself everything is ok, everything is fine; eventually, it will bite back.

Throughout the next six years our journey and relationship improved dramatically. Our unity had become extremely strong. Our relationship evolved into a togetherness you only witness in couples who have experienced 50 years of life together. We knew how and when each of us needed help; we knew what the other was thinking and what sort of day they had been through before walking in the front door. One thing that continued to deteriorate, no matter what we did, was Teri's health. Every week I was spending my days away from work with Teri visiting doctors, surgeons, physiotherapists, chiropractors, specialists and psychiatrists; in fact, anyone who could shed some light on why my wife spent eighty percent of her time wheelchair bound. The last visit we made to the hospital was to talk to the main specialist overlooking her case. The words that we heard were not what we expected. He sympathetically said they couldn't fix her, and as he continued, he explained that she had already tried every treatment they could offer, twice, and she was still regressing. The resulting impact of this statement on someone who is already suffering from a variety of mental health issues, along with the obvious physical problems, wasn't good. Teri dropped further into her hole. If her life, her temperament and her mental stability were on the edge before, this sent her over the top. Coming home after work was unbearable. I couldn't hold on for much longer. I was on the verge of leaving the family. Something had to change!

Whenever anything becomes continuously painful or uncomfortable, or any feeling of discomfort is felt for a prolonged period, either physically, mentally or spiritually, it creates change. It forces movement and an adaptation is required. This is the black and white of evolution. Muscles become stronger when they have been forced past what's comfortable; resilience develops only after you've been beaten to the ground time after time, and then only to ask for more, and it's only when you stand up in the face of adversity you learn how to build a wall to protect yourself from it. The amount of pain and discomfort we were feeling as individuals, and as a couple, forced a change. This firstly came in the form of a career change to a more manageable 40 hours a week office position. This gave me regular hours of nine to five, opening spare time to study. I studied because I refused to believe there was nothing that could be done to help my wife. There had to be something to explain why she couldn't function properly. What was the difference between her biology and mine? So, I began reading. The first logical step, for me anyway, was to educate myself about the human form and what made it tick. This progressed into books about nutrition, hydration, sleep patterns, stress management, mental health, anthropology, evolution, genetics and many other subjects. I can't count the number of books, documents, documentaries and podcasts I read and listened to over the next year or so.

Two people came into my life during this period, and they helped in different ways, but both equally as important to our future, and both becoming more than friends.

Mikey, whom I'd known for a few years previously as a work colleague, was on a journey of his own, thus bringing us closer together. We complemented each other's characters. I brought enthusiasm, support and adventure to the challenges we were each facing. Mikey would keep me grounded and level-headed, and eventually, greatly contributed to balancing my life, reducing my depression and anxiety issues. He now has his own studio where he teaches Tai Chi, mindfulness and martial arts.

I crossed paths with Karl through a friend of a friend when I was on a training weekend about building a successful Martial Arts business. I quickly realised he was also on a similar journey to me, but with a few more years of studying behind him. Everything I was looking for, and the answers to the questions I was asking, was already within Karl's vast knowledge, as he had devoured countless books on his quest for health and happiness. Another one of the biggest learning curves of my life was spending a week in Chamonix, France with Karl hiking through some of the most stunning scenery you could wish to behold on the planet. This was during the infancy of our relationship when I was hungry for information. I spent 14 hours every day during that mini adventure downloading information from Karl as he regurgitated hundreds of books. That week catapulted my understanding and awareness of the world around me, leaving me with a thirst for more. Karl now runs a business called 'Mother Nature's Diet' which has turned that week of knowledge in Chamonix into a company that helps educate others into living a healthier, happier life; not just for themselves, but for the planet as a whole. This has also been developed into a book entitled 'Mother Nature's Diet'.

After a year of building a library of books, documentaries and podcasts, both Teri and I realised "we" were living in a drastically wrong way: when I say "we", I mean we as the first world are unquestionably living the wrong way. The problems Teri and I were experiencing with our health were not isolated problems. An extremely large proportion of the population around us was developing similar issues. Diabetes, obesity, depression and anxiety are amongst many other health issues that are slowly becoming the norm in the western world. Realising this, we made some instant changes to lead a more primitive way of life, starting with our diet. We made a point of keeping more hydrated, exercised daily, breathed fresh air for at least an hour every day, maintained a regular sleep pattern, stopped drinking, stopped smoking, restricted social media interaction, and stopped listening to news feeds. Basically, we eliminated as many negative influences as possible, physically, nutritionally, emotionally and spiritually from our lives. The reaction to this was instantaneous. I lost 20kgs in weight, the boils on my skin cleared and the fog I lived with every day of my life lifted, relieving me from the depression I wasn't even aware of until it went; I felt lighter and walked taller. Teri's change was even more dramatic. Within three months she had no need for her wheelchair, then totally eliminated any need for any walking aids after a further three months. She was now capable of contributing to the world around us and giving me a much-needed reprieve from some of the household duties. Improvements in her mental health, similar to mine, very quickly encouraged smiles and laughter back into the family home.

Moving on to the present day, Teri now runs a successful Pet Care business, climbs and boulders once a week, rides horses, hikes over a variety of mountain ranges, and lives an extremely healthy and active lifestyle. We have two wonderful daughters who now have a mum they can interact with and share experiences with, and I have a wife with whom I can build an amazing memory bank. I'll say that again; I HAVE A WIFE! Not someone I look after, but a wife, and we have a great partnership. I now have someone I can share the same life experiences with, instead of leading two separate lives.

Over the past five years and with this new-found energy, passion, knowledge, drive and a few new qualifications, I have built a successful health club called 'SB Health & Fitness'. With the help of another very important addition to my world, Sylvia, this health club has become a place where people from all walks of life, all fitness levels and all health issues, both physical and mental, can come to feel safe, be open, and fight their own fight. We have an amazing community and support structure where the education is passed on, and hopefully, further on.

Sylvia first came into SB Health & Fitness as one of my clients looking for help and advice with training and nutrition. Everything she was looking to improve, soon improved. We became friends during a year of health coaching and started spending time with each other's families outside of the working environment. This led to a chain of challenges, concluding with Sylvia, her family and me, attempting the National 3-peaks. This is a very demanding 24-hour pursuit that requires you to hike the biggest mountains in Scotland, England and Wales, including the time it takes to drive the 462 miles between the mountains. Whilst travelling between Scafell Pike, the highest mountain in England, and Snowdon, the highest mountain in Wales, at 2 o'clock in the morning, listening to everyone else snoring like a chorus of bachelor frogs, I constructed a ridiculous idea of building SB Health and Fitness. Later that week I suggested to Sylvia that I honestly believed she needed a career change, far away from her twenty years as an Estate Agent. This wasn't an unselfish suggestion, because I wanted her to become the Manager of SB Health and Fitness. After she stopped laughing, I disclosed my plan. I told her I had complete confidence in her and her ability to adapt. She then signed on the dotted line and went to college for retraining. I am a firm believer in the right people, not the right qualifications. You can educate anybody, but you can't change their character, and Sylvia was unquestionably the person for the job.

So, as you can see, I have had a few issues that needed to be overcome; although, nothing too dramatic. I haven't been made an orphan or come from a physically abusive family or come from a deprived third world country or even been overly bullied. There are millions of people who would dream of having an upbringing like mine. But some of the events and the situations I have experienced, and some of the people that have influenced me have left a few scars. This could sound much like anybody's story, and I think that's the point of the book. I'm hoping you can relate to me throughout my writing, with the understanding that anyone can grow, learn and adapt to any situation. You don't have to be a marine, a movie star, an Olympian, a homeowner, a director, or even popular, to be successful. If you can close your eyes every day before you sleep with the knowledge that you had a successful day, believing you achieved your goals or learnt from your failures, then that day is inevitably a progression. How powerful, how involved, and how present in your own life could you be if every single day of your life you progress, learn and evolve?

Chapter 3
Round 1

BANG! A few grunts and cheers and we're off, marching forward along the Dempster Highway with nothing but a couple of small towns separating us from Tuktoyaktuk (Tuk), the finish line of the 6633 at the Arctic Ocean. Well, when I say nothing, there is the 352 miles, 4000+ meters of ascent, -40 degrees Celsius, katabatic winds, and the harsh, extreme, inhospitable, lonely wilderness of the Arctic Circle, we will be painstakingly jogging, walking and crawling over for the next week or so.

2013 was the 6th edition of the event. There were two disciplines; a 120-mile race to Fort McPherson and the 350-mile race to Tuktoyaktuk. The 350 is considered in many books and reports as one of the most difficult. It's very deserving of its title: 'The toughest, coldest, windiest ultra-distance foot race on the planet'. During the first seven years, which included the finishers of the 2013 event, only twelve people had finished the race from one hundred plus participants. Competitors are self-sufficient for the entirety of the event, dragging with them everything they need to survive on a sled; food, clothing, first aid, sled repairs, hygiene, etc., with the only outside assistance being water, that is supplied at each of the eight checkpoints.

There is also a strict, challenging time limit of eight days allocated to complete the route. An hour is even taken away because you travel through different time zones between the Yukon and the Northern Territories.

Checkpoints are: -

CP1 Arctic circle at 23 miles

CP2 James Creek at 69 miles
CP3 Fort McPherson at 116 miles
CP4 Tsiigehtchic at 154 miles
CP5 Caribou Creek at 205 miles
CP6 Inuvik at 235 miles
CP7 Swimming Point at 305 miles
CP8 Tuktoyaktuk at 352 miles

As Martin fired the gun to start the athletes at the truck stop, it snapped me back to the present like a click of the finger's inches away from my ear. I suddenly felt alive; every sense became alert; I could hear the adrenaline-fuelled deep breathing from the competitors around me like charging horses. I spotted minuscule avalanches of snow cascading down the branches on the trees as we passed by, and I felt every pebble, stone or ripple in the thin compacted snow blanketing the tarmac. This is it; this is what I was here for, and this is the answer to everyone's first question, when describing the race to those back home... WHY? Why do you feel the need to do this? The answer...TO FEEL ALIVE.

The first 10 km from Eagle Plains took us through a majestic woodland as we slowly descended all the way down to a cast iron cantilever bridge carrying us over the Eagle River. I was amazingly comfortable at this stage, progressing steadily to near the front of the pack with only David Berridge in front of me, as he determinedly headed towards Tuk. This was his second attempt after failing early on a few years before. Kevin Hollings was the only other athlete in front who had created a huge gap as he was headed for the 120-mile race record. I was surprisingly impressed with the distance that I had created behind me from the other athletes. But the euphoria wasn't to last for long. From the bridge, the road ascends progressively for the next 10 km's, and, with the road surface changing to a more weather haggard, ice-damaged mish mash, the going wasn't so easy. Sometimes smooth tarmac, other times patched with ice and, more often than not, the surface became very loose and gritty, making dragging the sled more of a challenge. This was when the acceptance of my first mistake wormed its way into my thoughts, creating a tidal wave of negativity. The sled I was dragging from my hips by a harness was, without mixing my words, shit. Looking back, I guess I knew that the moment I hitched up. This quickly prompted the realisation of my second mistake. I couldn't make it through this event driven by my ego and stubbornness, like every other race I had entered. I felt a very virtual slap around the face. This was the moment I admitted to myself I hadn't a bloody clue what I was doing. I hadn't built a suitable CV or gathered the right experience, understanding and expertise to warrant standing on this road.

I wasn't even supposed to be in the Canadian Arctic. I was supposed to be on Lake Baikal in Siberia competing in the first ever Black Ice Race. In July 2012 I had a sudden burst of invincibility, or stupidity, and signed up for this totally different race in Siberia, with a company called 'Extreme World Races'. We were to race from the southernmost point of Lake Baikal to the northernmost point, traveling 420 miles on the ice. This Black Ice Race is the adventure that was devouring my every thought for over seven months building up to February 2013. I spent days and weeks mentally accepting the challenges ahead, visualising different scenarios as I read book after book about the area, the climate and the culture. Unfortunately, the race was cancelled four weeks before departure and I was left with a hole to fill; the 6633 was my rebound race. Just like in any relationship, the rebound is never a good place to start. I say it was unfortunately cancelled, but looking back, I am so thankful I didn't go to Siberia. The Black Ice Race would have chewed me up and spat me out

- another place where the geography and weather had no time for ego. Ego can get you killed when you assume you can beat Mother Nature. You can't; you need to roll with the punches and hope she lets you walk out.

So, with six months' worth of pent-up energy, enthusiasm and visualisation, the release that I needed from competing in The Black Ice Race was taken away and I was left rocking on the end of my bed, tormented. Within a couple of days, I was reading about the 6633 Ultra. I found it by typing 'the hardest races on the planet' into the search engine, then after a quick phone call and a visit to meet Martin in Wales I was signed up. I couldn't believe my luck. It was to take place at the same time of the year, so no need to change any work plans. "Result!", I whispered to myself as I drove away from Martin's house. Canada was a totally different race, needing different equipment in a different environment with different rules, and I had signed up on the rebound a few weeks before departure. What could go wrong? After convincing Martin I was competent enough to compete, I mentioned I needed a sled, but with only four weeks until take-off at Heathrow Airport, I couldn't organise one. He reassured me that when arriving at Race HQ in Whitehorse there would be some sleds left over from previous races, so plenty of options for me to choose from. He was partially right. There was one! it was this one; this train wreck of a sled I was fighting with up the incline from Eagle River. The poles that attached to the harness around my waist replicated in look, feel and weight, to scaffolding poles instead of the thin lightweight aluminium poles that would normally connect athletes to their sleds. This made it, obviously, less than ideal, with no give, very solid and ridiculously weighty on the hips. It also created an uneven pivot point across the wheels placed in the middle of the length of this beast, creating an angle between the sled and road that was very much off the optimal parallel. The back end of the sled glided a centimetre or two off the floor, causing it to make slight contact with the surface of the road every 15 to 20 steps. The magnitude of these slight jolts multiplied once I started ascending and continued increasing with the infrequent stability of the frost-damaged tarmac. Through stubbornness and ignorance, I continued fighting forward trying to keep up with David and keep him within my sights.

At mile 23 we reach the first checkpoint. This is the shortest distance between checkpoints but an essential stop. This is where you pass the latitude of the Arctic Circle sitting at 66 degrees 33 minutes and 39 seconds north, and why the race is named the 6633 Ultra. Standing next to the large surreal Arctic Circle sign in the middle of absolutely nowhere is the photo opportunity of the race. Approaching this sign with the mobile trailer of a checkpoint placed in front of it at 712 meters above sea level, you get a true appreciation of the vastness of your surroundings. My mind wasn't on the beauty of the location though; my mind was focused on the ever-increasing pain and restriction of movement slowly developing in my right hip. Every time the rear end of the sled smacked, grazed or brushed the iced asphalt, it sent a shudder through the steel poles vibrating against my hips. A few hundred yards from this temporary reprieve of the checkpoint I could see David leaving. Time to regain some lost distance, I thought. Naively thinking this sled problem was only a temporary setback, I believed it would either correct itself all on its own or I would just become attuned to it. So, with a quick mandatory picture by the sign and some hot water added to my dry-frozen lunch, I quickly shuffled on, deliberately moving forward with a slight bend in my knees to prevent the continued bullying from the sled. With the distraction of a warm chicken teriyaki, and David back in view, the torment of the sled went away. This was unfortunately short-lived. From the Arctic Circle to an unofficial checkpoint called Rock River twenty-six miles later, and with the road being described as undulating, it wasn't long before the sled was the number one villain again. *Undulating*. This word always makes me chuckle when event organisers describe a race as undulating. Mountainous is a more accurate description, rolling higher and higher, becoming more and more exposed. This area is known as hurricane alley, famous for its potential to have extremely high winds known as katabatic winds. You see, it's the winds that create the danger; it's the winds that kill people. -20 or -30 degrees Celsius is quite do-able with some quality clothing but add a 40-mph wind and things can change; things become deadly. -20 degrees C with a 40-mph wind gives a wind chill of -57 degrees C, and similarly, -30 degrees will feel like -71 with a 40-mph wind.

These winds commonly hit 40-50 mph, occasionally hitting 70-80 mph and regularly blow trucks onto their side. They bring any human to their knees, searching for refuge in any hole they can find for survival. They come from nowhere and disappear just as quickly. Fortunately for me, this wasn't on the agenda today. It was very calm, eerie and cold, around -36 degrees C. The darkness of the first night quickly moved in, bringing with it a loneliness and vulnerability I had never felt before. All kinds of demons infiltrated my conscience, imagining worsening case scenarios. I was hoping to waddle into Rock River before bedding down for the night, but with the monkey in my head inventing argument after argument, and my hip feeling like I had been driven into from the side, I pulled over for the night a few miles short. Dropping off very quickly, I was sharply woken within an hour by one of the event organisers driving past for a check-up. He ordered me to move further away from the road for safety, before continuing to drive on. The pain that travelled from my right hip to my foot instantly forced a scream that started from the depths of my stomach, as I tried to guide myself out of the bivvy to obey the organiser's request. I knew from that moment it was game over. That was the moment I knew I had lost the fight with the scaffold poles. With tears in my eyes and a cold sweat creeping over me, I managed to drag my bivvy to a safer distance and scrambled back in. I was in a state of panic, every inch of my being shivering uncontrollably, praying that someone would come past soon so I didn't have to die. This was one of those scenes in a movie when you witness the actor, whose life is on the line, assess their life. What have I left behind? How is this going to affect loved ones? Two hours passed. I couldn't move, and every twitch sent a shockwave of pain down my leg. With dangerously low temperatures, uncontrollable shaking and the realistic chance that this could be it, all I could think of was Teri and the girls, and why am I doing this to them. Why do I continue to do this to myself; when will I ever learn? Another hour of silence passed before I could hear the shuffling of feet and the crunching of snow. I shouted out for help, receiving a muffled reply of "What do you need?". Begging with a quivering voice, to instantly send help back from the next checkpoint.

A lifetime later I imagined hearing voices, followed by being dragged by my shoulders from the sleeping bag. Hours later, waking up in the back of a trailer, I realised it wasn't my imagination. Scott the medic was in the trailer treating the already damaged feet of another racer. Noticing I was conscious he asked if I was ok, and did I want anything? Standing up I remembered why I was there. I still felt like I'd been the victim of a hit and run. Scott was a tough, no-holds-barred, straight-talking ex-forces medic who instantly made me feel insecure and unworthy, especially with an injury so early into the race, so I replied, "I'll be ok after a few tablets and some food."

"Will it be ok to continue with the race?" I continued desperately.

At the break of dawn, I was deposited at the exact point I had been saved from the night before, sled and backpack still in the same position but frozen solid. I harnessed myself back into the scaffold poles, took a deep breath and took a step forward, then another and another. I was in the race once again. One mile became another, and it wasn't too long before I passed Rock River. With a glimmer of hope, I headed towards Wright Pass, but once again, with the very slightest incline, the weight of the steel bars instantly angered my hips causing me to drag my right foot behind. My leg felt as if it was a dead, useless piece of flesh, a dead weight. The last thing I needed was more weight to drag over Wright Pass. Wright Pass, some would say, can be the hardest, most exposed section of the race. The directors of the 6633 have been forced in previous years to apply contingency plans to the event because of the aggressive, undisputable 70-80 mph winds, or the six, eight or even ten feet of snow dropped there the previous day. Wright Pass was the next obstacle I needed to overcome, and an obstacle I started to understand was beyond my capabilities, especially with a limb that didn't want to be part of this race, or even part of me anymore.

I did manage to scramble, grunt, cry and drag my way to the start of Wright Pass, 15 miles further along from Rock River, before I hit the crusty tarmac and met the floor with my face. My right leg refused point blank to be placed in a supporting role. There wasn't a hope in hell it was going to be placed on the ice one more time. Every movement in any direction felt like a surgical implement was forcing the ball of my thigh bone out of its socket in my hip. I managed to get back to my feet...sorry...foot and using my walking poles as crutches, I tried hopping forward, still dragging the sled with me. Every time I hopped forward the pain would multiply; every third or fourth hop I would slip and fall. As you can imagine, it didn't take long before the monkey in my head did the calculations and explained it was impossible to finish this race if my cruising speed was half a mile per hour. With this, and with my guts wrenched out, I threw in the towel, spending the next twenty minutes trying to squirm into the sleeping bag to wait for help. Within the hour I was collected and moved forward to Fort McPherson. This is where I spent the next couple of nights, slowly slipping into a very dark place, unable to move and no one to talk to, most importantly my wife. If I ever needed the connection with Teri, it was now. I needed to feel her touch, I needed to hear her voice, I needed her comfort, but I was alone.

Believe it or not, Wi-Fi wasn't a common thing in 2013, especially in such a vast expanse of nothingness. There was no phone connection or even the ability to send a message. The only connection I had with home was some letters I had asked Teri, the girls and a couple of mates to write for me. These had been stuffed into a sealed envelope for use when times grew hard. Well, it was now bloody hard, and I must have read those letters 50 times over in the following days. I lived in those letters.

My days then progressed into a roller coaster of the same emotions and events, which always started with waking up, trying to understand where I was, then painfully rediscovering I had an incredibly angry hip. I would then stock up on nutrition and hydration along with a cocktail of drugs. Next came the music through my Sony Walkman and the reading of the letters. This served two purposes. Firstly, to disconnect as many senses as possible from my current position and surroundings, and secondly to create a state of depression that would lead to tears which would help me back to sleep. I still sleep when I'm depressed now, preferring the dream world to reality. This cycle repeated itself about every four hours. Every time I woke up, I prayed another day was over and that I was a day closer to going home, but no. It was just another four to five hours farther along the same day.

Letter from Teri

Hi my cuddly Bear...I love you.

This is it, you're actually there, doing it! All the training and hard work you've put in over the last few years to finally put it to good use, to achieve one of your dreams. I'm very proud of your dedication. I just wish I could be there with you to share your dream.

You know that I'll be missing you like crazy and thinking of you every day and night, and will be desperately trying to track your progress.

You know that I'll probably have changed the house around, or built a wall somewhere, or even taken one down. You know what I'm like with my little projects.

I guess if you're reading this you've probably hit a bit of a wall. You know you have the mental strength to achieve this and can get to the end. You've proved that with the Coast to Coast challenge. Just know that you have a lot of people here that love and care for you, and are very proud of you. You have the physical strength to do this. Just focus on one step at a time and think of the big hugs you're going to get from me at the airport.

I'll be lying in bed every night thinking of you fighting through the cold wind and snow. I'll be with you every step of the way, every step you take I'll be there right beside you.

Dig deep babe. Every step takes you closer to achieving your dream.

I love you Bear. Come home safe xxxx

Letter from Myia aged 11

To daddy

Have a good time. I hope you can take lots of pictures to show us and we all miss you lots :-) :-) xx :-) :-) xxxxxxxx

Proud of you and don't stop walking daddy.

Love you

See you soon xxxxx

Letter from Keira aged 8

Dear Daddy xx

I miss you lots and lots xx

I love you so much daddy xx

Don't stop walking daddy xx

I'm very proud of you xx

Have a lovely time xx

Lots of love xx

I can't even copy the letters into the book without bringing the tears back.

From Fort McPherson I was moved to Inuvik. The DNFs (Did Not Finish) needed to move along the course as the race progressed. We were now five days into the race with only six athletes left, being led by David Berridge and followed by Ian Hall who was twelve hours behind. As already mentioned, this was David's second attempt at the race, and being a very experienced veteran of the multistage ultra-race, he had returned to finish something he had started. He has an outstanding catalogue of accomplishments ranging from cold, jungle and desert races to single day 100 milers and he even ran 100 miles within 24 hours on a treadmill. I couldn't think of anything worse than spending that long on a treadmill. A very inspirational guy who has written a couple of books about his adventures; 'Fartleks and Flatulence' and 'The Runners Nuts'. Definitely worth a look.

Inuvik is probably the most luxurious of all the checkpoints. The chalet-type accommodation supplied a proper bed, heated rooms, hot showers and a small kitchen. These were available for all to use, athletes and DNFs alike, although the athletes took priority, obviously. This didn't bother me because the hole I was mentally wallowing in refused the comfort and chose to hide on the floor in the corner feeling sorry for myself.

Inuvik itself is also the largest stopover. It has a few shops, pubs, restaurants and even a nightclub, so it offered the best opportunity to find a way of speaking to Teri. So, with a wobble, a shuffle and a drag around the stores, I found a way to purchase some international calling credit on my prehistoric Nokia 3310, which gave me 30 minutes of talk time, it wasn't much, but it was enough to find a quiet isolated part of town and sob uncontrollably to her. Looking back, it must have been so heart-wrenching for Teri. She really wanted to help me, to take care of me, but must have felt so helpless. To this day, it was one of the hardest goodbyes I've ever said.

Sue Likey is Martin's wife and known for being the mother hen of the support team. Whilst the entirety of the support crew had a responsibility to the runners still on the ice, and rightly so, Sue was the person to go to if you needed a talk or a shoulder. Numerous times she would grab my attention to see if I would like anything or a chat, but I refused repeatedly. She is a particularly important member of the team and an easy person to talk to, but not for me in this mindset. Being a veteran in ultra-running, she understood everyone had their own healing process. She had built a respectable CV of events alongside Martin before retiring from competition, and then developing the 6633 in 2007, amongst other races, more local to Wales.

On the edge of the Arctic Ocean stands a small settlement called Tuktoyaktuk (Tuk), 352 miles from Eagle Plains. Tuk has a small, very friendly and welcoming community of fewer than 1000 locals, built historically around the natural harbour and covering a landmass of 5.4 sq miles. This was the supply chain for the rest of the local communities. In current years income relies more on tourism, although many still live traditionally with plenty of residents still making a livelihood from hunting, fishing and trapping. The local school consisted of one large-ish hall, a kitchen and a shower/toilet room. This was my home for the next few days, as the last racers slowly inhabited the space around me. Four inspiring, very impressive individuals managed to overcome this life-changing challenge in 2013. David Berridge, Ian Hall, Dean Clifford and Pete Hawkins. Very inspiring efforts from all, but still I had no energy or enthusiasm left to give them during their finest hour.

The last evening at Tuk before leaving for the long arduous journey home, I'd decided to wake up before dawn and shuffle onto the Arctic Ocean with the idea of leaving the area with some sort of a positive memory. I managed to limp far enough away from Tuk that it was barely noticeable as a village. I sat down on the frozen virgin snow blanketing the sea and waited, contented, until the sun rose. I did try and make myself a bowl of porridge with some boiling water I had carried with me in the flask, but it froze solid by the time I had replaced the top on the flask. The spectrum of colours the sky went through as the sun woke up, just for me, was hypnotising. It was truly magnificent. For the first, and only time during the journey I felt torn up, believing I would never see this place again.

Retracing our steps back to Whitehorse was agonising. But at least I was heading towards my world for the first time in two weeks. Three flights later, as the wheels touched down back at Heathrow, I couldn't move quickly enough to get through the last hurdles separating me from everything I had been dreaming of: the three most important people in my life. As my eyes scanned the terminal, I grabbed a glimpse of them between the hustle of bodies. I moved with gazelle-like speed to get to them... probably looked more like an injured sloth in reality...but instantly felt safe as we all embraced each other and I whispered into Teri's ear, "I promise never to leave you again."

Famous last words!

Chapter 4
The Road to Nowhere

Answering a couple of those recurring questions that were floating around my head when I was travelling through the freezer in Canada, was the first stage of my recovery. How did I get there in the first place? And why did I feel I was competent enough to take on such a challenge? I guess this journey started when I began driving trucks.

Passing my HGV (Heavy Goods Vehicle) licence in 2007, and driving the articulated trucks for ASDA was, I believed at the time, the best possible thing that could have happened. Our family was going through a difficult time. We were earning less than we were spending month after month. I was working seven days most weeks and up to 12 hours a day, just trying to keep the red letters from coming through the door. Teri's health was declining rapidly, we were arguing constantly about money, and ignorantly, I wasn't giving our daughters any of the quality time they needed. Then, I qualified as a truck driver – 50% more income, more days off, better shift patterns and more time to help at home, initially anyway. Everything improved...apart from my health. Within six months of driving, my weight had increased by three and a half stone (roughly 22 kilos) and I couldn't understand why. I was eating less than I did previously as a Team Leader in the warehouse. It didn't matter how much I reduced my calorie intake, I continued to gain weight. At the time, I didn't have the knowledge I have now, so I just assumed it was a lack of movement. I didn't know much about exercise, hormones, macros, sleep patterns, or stress management. The only way I knew how to exercise as a child was through football. So, I spread the word around fellow colleagues to see if I could entice any of the other oldies to join me, once a week, for some five-a-side football in the town sports hall. It makes me chuckle now to think I classed mid-thirties as oldies, especially now I'm 47 years old and can run rings around most 20-year-olds. I was pleasantly surprised with the response, realising I was not the only driver worried about their health.

Every Tuesday evening, I would rent the hall for an hour, and between 10 and 20 guys would turn up. This is when and how Gyula became part of my world. He was a fantastic footballer and always the first one picked for a team. Before leaving Hungary, he was a semi-pro goalkeeper, so he very quickly became our star player. After a couple of teams had been thrown together, we would proceed to run around like headless chickens for the first fifteen minutes, before one by one, reducing ourselves to quivering, lightheaded, nauseous wrecks. By the end of the hour, we resembled a pile of overweight, dehydrated, dizzy, weak, emasculated apes, trying to hold onto any thread of our youth and respect. At least, that's what I felt like. I was 34 years old and presumed this must be what it feels like to be 34, after all, when you're 16, 34 is viewed as old; and now I felt it. These Tuesday night kickabouts didn't last for long; maybe for a few months before the group became smaller and smaller.

From what I understand now, I believe the discomfort we felt after each game picked them off one by one. It's quite easy to be influenced by the other voice in your head which shouts louder when you know the discomfort you are feeling is connected to the task you really should be doing, but don't want to do. I guess most of them found other things that were significantly more important right at that moment, like watching football or ironing, or just using the excuse of a hard day at work. So, the final whistle went on that and I was back to my sedentary life.

My need to find an alternative means of exercise fell on Gyula's shoulders. The Tuesday after we closed the doors on the football, he turned up at my door with an amazingly stupid idea of going for a run around the town. After a little bullying from him and a couple of coffees, we ventured out for my first ever 5 km jog. I wore a casual t-shirt, a pair of old fleece joggers that were cut to the thighs, and my indoor football trainers which had the flexibility of tyre iron. The first half a mile was fantastic; I thought I had missed my calling. The second half a mile wasn't so elegant, and by the end of the second mile, sickness and dehydration came, followed by hyperventilation and dizziness. That first 5 km took me 44 minutes. I could have walked the bloody thing quicker. But with Gyula's persistence, this became part of our week, eventually bringing the same route down to a respectable 30 minutes. I even bought a treadmill to cover a few miles between outings.

After a couple of years lifting weights, studying martial arts and steadily increasing mileage on my runs, exercise had comfortably developed into a habit, to the point that, if I missed a day, I wouldn't be nice to live with. I guess I would go as far as say, it was an addiction more than a habit. I wouldn't say I was strong or fit or healthy; I didn't really know what I was doing. I just needed to do something every day. There was no rhyme or reason to my training; I just knew I loved the feeling of being completely hammered and I was constantly looking for more. I needed a challenge, a focus, and a reason. After a steady Saturday morning run and with a coffee in hand, me and my partner-in-crime Gyula, set out to find an adventure. What about going high? I suggested. "What's the biggest mountain in the UK?" I asked. Ben Nevis in Scotland, the search engine replied. That's it, Ben Nevis; let's conquer the biggest mountain we could find. Four weeks later, and after an expensive trip to the local outdoor adventure shop for a pair of new boots, a jacket, rucksack, socks, hat, gloves and everything else you would need for a two-week trek along the Himalayas, me, Gyula, and a new addition, Andre, were heading for Scotland. Andre, a Slovakian, and a work colleague of Gyula's, just happened to have the weekend off and thought he would tag along.

Never experiencing a youth hostel before, the three nights were an adventure in themself. The weekend materialised into a lads' weekend away, but with two days of hiking thrown in, both days crowning the top of Ben Nevis. We felt like explorers, laying down the footsteps for future generations to follow. It wasn't important that there were many other souls grafting up and down throughout the weekend. It was our mountain, and just like any other successful expedition, we celebrated in style. That night we each devoured a whole pre-cooked chicken, a loaf of bread and a jar of pickled gherkins, washed down with a few beers and what can only be described as paint thinners, was actually a Hungarian drink called Palinka which is 88% proof and 37.5% alcohol, also known as moonshine. It wasn't long before Andre had passed out, leaving the two of us giggling like schoolboys. Then nature called, because what goes in, must come out, and with this being a hostel, the toilets were communal. So, as quietly as two drunken schoolboys could be, we tiptoed down the corridor wearing nothing but our boxers, did our business and tiptoed back. It was, after all, one o'clock in the morning, and the hostel was full. Reaching the now-locked door to our room and with no key, panic set in. No matter how loud we whispered, Andre was in dreamland. We were on our own, in boxers, in a strange hostel, in the middle of Fort William. It was early March, and it was snowing outside. Remembering we had left the window to our room slightly open, we crept downstairs and out the front door to find our window along the side of the building. It was bloody freezing, but we had no choice. The window stood about ten feet/three meters from the ground. The only way to acquire access to it would be for one of us to stand on the other's shoulders. I have no idea how we managed this, being barefoot and with a bottle of paint thinners in our blood, but with some obvious natural gymnastic capabilities, we did. Gyula was standing on my shoulders whispering as loud as he could to wake Andre. It was at this precise moment the owner of the hostel burst through the back door with a baseball bat in his hand, screaming with a broad Scottish accent "I'm gonna beat the shit out of you, you wee bastards, come err". With that, we were gone. I still believe I made it to the end of the driveway with Gyula still attached to my shoulders, with the landlord still in pursuit. It was below freezing, we were being chased down a street in Scotland in our underwear and drunk, by an angry Scotsman with a baseball bat believing we were attempting to break into his house. Eventually, by shouting over our shoulders, we made him understand who we were. So, like a pair of escaped convicts, we were marched back to our room. The rest of the weekend followed a similar path, creating an array of humorous stories on our triumphant return back to civilization.

Sitting in my lounge laughing as we enthusiastically recalled every one of the stories during our expedition, the question inevitably arose - what next? We had mastered height, in our little worlds; what about distance?

My mother-in-law managed a charity called RoSA (Rape or Sexual Abuse). The charity provides a valuable service helping survivors who have suffered indescribable assaults. I offered to raise some much-needed funds by taking part in an event called 'Just Walk'. A 60 km hike along the South Downs; an amazingly scenic path that ran west to east between Southern London and the coast. In May of 2011, Gyula and I stood with another 2000 people ready to take on this challenge that was unfathomable to us only a couple of months before. It still scared the crap out of us, especially as this was the first time I had ever stood on the starting line of anything. But what's the worst that could happen, I thought? I can't remember much of the event, apart from the fact that nine and a half hours later we crossed the finish line like a pair of Frankenstein's, unable to bend, cramping from muscles we never knew we had, and barefoot as we had bought boots that were lovely and snuggly at the beginning, but didn't allow room for swelling, so took them off. Believe it or not, we crossed the finish in first and second place, one and a half hours quicker than the record. How was this possible? We won! Wow...Now, don't get carried away, this was a walking event, nothing Olympian, but we had won. The emotion driving home was addictive; I felt I could do anything. I needed more, so what next? Arriving back in Lutterworth, still passionately discussing the next challenge, we pulled up outside the local pizzeria. Both of us were expecting the other to jump out and collect some well-deserved food. However quickly realising neither of us could move, we rang the takeaway we were currently parked outside and placed the order, arranging for them to deliver it through the window of our car.

This feeling of being broken started to become a need. I wasn't sure why, but I was developing an addiction to it. Just like any other addiction, the need to satisfy it grew bigger, requiring me to look for further, harder challenges to break me in the same way.

It wasn't long before the need took over again: what was next? I don't think I lasted more than a month before the hunger grew and I needed a fix. Something we could do without too much preparation, money, or time off work. The one thing that jumped out after hearing a discussion over the canteen floor by some colleagues at work, was a challenge named the 3-Peaks Challenge. A 24-hour time limit to ascend and descend the highest peaks in three countries: Ben Nevis in Scotland, which we were already familiar with, Scafell Pike in England, and Snowdon in Wales. I was more than comfortable with Snowdon, having peaked it a couple of times before from previous weekends away with friends. Scafell Pike took some research to find where to start and the best route when on a quick timescale. With a long weekend free from work and a twist of the arm in Gyula's direction, we were packed for our mini adventure, not yet seven weeks after we had finished 'Just Walk'. When I say packed, it was once again naively planned. In my head, this is how I envisaged it going. Seven o'clock Friday morning we would leave my home in Lutterworth, hopefully covering the 425 miles to the base of Ben Nevis in Fort William by 3pm. Take an hour to rest, grab some food and a coffee before starting the challenge at 4pm. This would then give us until 4pm on Saturday to finish our descent of Snowdon in Wales. Grab a couple of hours sleep in the car before shooting back the 150 miles home, falling into bed by 10pm. Perfect, no accommodation needed and only one day holiday used, leaving the whole of Sunday to recover. Thursday evening, I grabbed clothing for cold, warm and wet weather, a couple of pairs of shoes, a head torch, as well as food and drink.

Food consisted of chocolate bars and Ginster steak pasties. Drink came in two crates: one crate of 12 bottles of water and the other 12 cans of Red Bull.

This, as you probably know, is not the best nutrition to get through 1,000 miles of driving, 10,000 feet of ascent, 26 miles laterally on foot, and at most, two hours sleep within a 40-hour period: but a lesson needed to be learned.

As planned, seven o'clock the next morning we drove north, and true to plan, hit Ben Nevis car park eight hours later feeling slightly tired and a little dizzy from being in constant motion for the equivalent of a working day. After we had a coffee, a steak slice and a Red Bull, the clock started counting down the 24 hours as we left at 4pm on the dot. It was a glorious day, mid 20 degree Celsius and blue skies. Yep, I had to double-check myself that we were still in Scotland. Ten months before, when we summited Ben Nevis for the first time, we looked like adventurers with a sack on our back full of equipment for any possible outcome, which is why it probably took us eight hours. This time couldn't have been further from that image. We were only armed with 500ml of water each, and enough caffeine and ego to battle through any situation. We were cruising up the 1352 meters ascent from the car park to the peak like a pair of possessed Neanderthals, dressed in shorts, a t-shirt and a bandana. Once standing on the top, we paused just long enough to take a few photos. It needed to be done; the view was something I have never seen the like of before. Sea on one side as far as the sky and surrounded in the other direction by the pinnacles of every mountain top of the Grampian range. I have since revisited Ben eight times and have never seen that perfect view again. Charging down the 5.25-mile path passing everyone we had waved to on the way up, and receiving some strange looks as we did, we stood back in the car park three hours and fifteen minutes after we had left. Minutes later, with food stuffed in our cheeks, resembling a couple of six-foot chipmunks, and a couple of caffeine drinks stored in the side doors of the car to give us wings, we set off to our next target 257-miles away in England.

Scafell Pike is slap bang in the middle of the Lake District and not very quick to navigate to. Arriving at 1.20am, six hours later, we jumped out and powered the best we could up the mountain from the Wasdale Car Park.

It was dark, clear-skied, with only a small crest of a moon. As usual, relying on my extensive experience, we only purchased the most basic of head torches. I'm pretty confident in saying that a jar full of fireflies would have done a better job and as mentioned before, I really felt uncomfortable in the dark, especially when the eyes of the sheep reflected back at us from our torches as if they were demons stalking us in the darkness. Put it this way, I was so relieved that Gyula was with me. The job needed doing and it did get done, in a steady three hours and twenty-five minutes. Considering neither of us had ever been to the Lake District before, and it was the middle of the night, we were both pleased with the result. Another 8 miles and 978 meters ascended. But fatigue was setting in – 23 hours since our eyes last closed - we were about to embark on another 250-mile journey to Pen-y-Pas car park, with only Snowdon itself to manoeuvre ourselves over. I guess the only thing for it was a couple of our Ginsters specials, flushed down with a couple more tins of caffeine before leaving the Lake District.

The first hour after leaving Wasdale was probably the most frightening hour of driving I have ever experienced. Sheep all over the roads, twists, turns, deep fog, roads so narrow the wing mirrors would touch bushes on both sides at the same time, and hazy eyes. Entering the motorway lifted the stress off the shoulders and we both relaxed a little. Adding to that, we were just under three hours ahead of schedule. Parking up at Snowdon, we had lost an hour of our advantage by sitting in traffic caused by an accident just outside Manchester, but that was out of our control and it was part of the game. Once again, standing next to our car at 10am in shorts, t-shirts and armed with a 500ml bottle of water, we decided to chase the 20-hour finish time. That means we only had two hours to smash Snowdon. We were gone, like a pair of ferrets up the Pyg path, summited Snowdon an hour and

15 minutes later. Still with the chequered flag in our sights, and the thought of finishing this underestimated, under-planned and under-trained adventure, we bolted back down the miners' path along the side of the two lakes and into the car park, stopping the watch with 3 hours 50 minutes left on the clock. We had done the National 3-peaks in an incredible 20 hours and 10 minutes. What glory, what triumph, what joy and pride we must have felt!... nope; it was one of the worst feelings I have felt. The adrenaline stopped, the pressure was released, and I felt destroyed. It wasn't anything physically; my muscles felt tired but nothing I hadn't felt before on numerous occasions. I felt extremely tired, but I've done long stints before whilst working; this wasn't anything new. I felt a mixture of depression, anger, grief, disappointment, solitude and aggression. I didn't want to be where I was or anywhere else for that matter. I didn't want company but felt anger when no one was close. I didn't want to sleep but felt frustrated that I was still awake. I just wanted to get home, so I dominantly told Gyula to get in the car, we're going. "Going where", he replied. "We're going home, right now." Three hours later and without a word said during the journey, I was dropping my adventuring buddy back at his home before parking up outside mine.

I sat on my own in the car for a lifetime, without a shred of emotion left, analysing what had just happened. I had just done the National 3-peaks Challenge in 20 hours and 10 minutes without a minute of sleep. The whole process used up only 32 hours and 30 minutes of my life, door to door. A thousand miles of driving, 10,000 feet of ascent and a marathon fuelled on pasties and Red Bull. What the .... had just happened? Looking back, that was 50% incredible, and 50% pure stupidity. What the bloody hell was I thinking? Even though the challenge was once again smashed; now, I accept the challenge was a total failure. It was a perfect lesson on how not to do something.

Unlocking the front door of my home to the surprise of Teri, who was not expecting to see me for at least another 12 hours, I marched straight past her and the girls to the bedroom where I spent the remainder of the weekend, continuing to ignore everyone, wallowing in my own pit of stupidity. I remember that hole I was in lasted for weeks. It wasn't until years later that I understood how damaging the lack of sleep, especially accompanied with fatigue and a diabolical diet can seriously affect hormonal balances and, in turn, affect mood. If there is one thing you must learn from this book, it's 'don't climb mountains on sugar and caffeine'.

It wasn't long before usual protocol kicked back in and I was looking for something bigger. Ben Nevis wasn't enough, 'Just Walk' wasn't enough, the National 3-peaks rocked me a bit, but I could do more. It was the middle of January and I was feeling the usual January blues and needed a fix. It was back to the search engines for the weekend. What could I find bigger than the 3-peaks that didn't cost the earth and sounded intimidating? After browsing through a variety of races and events, I stumbled across a link for a famous walking or cycling route stretching across England called Coast to Coast. This 192-mile path starts at a small village called St Bees on the Coastal part of the Lake District. Travelling east, passing straight over the Lake District and through the Yorkshire Dales; over the top of the Yorkshire Moors and finishing in the busy holiday town of Robin Hood's Bay. Sounds promising, I thought; this needs further research. Apparently, if you class yourself as a stroller, allocate 17-ish days to make it across the country. If you have good walking legs go for 14 days, but if you are very active, fit and can hold a consistent strong march, maybe you could be looking at between 10 to 12 days. I couldn't use two weeks' worth of holiday for my selfish hobby. That wouldn't be fair on Teri and the girls. There must be an alternative. Continued research showed that around ten thousand people hike the route each year, but there is a small group of strange individuals that attempt the trek in five days, known as the five dayers. These add up to less than one percent of the hikers each year. This has now got my interest. Five days, 192-miles, and as self-sufficient as possible to keep costs down; that sounds ridiculous. Perfect. This was my next fix. Just one more equally tough challenge to go before this 'Coast to Coast' could be marked in the calendar. I had to pick up the phone and call Gyula; I needed my wingman. When he answered I blurted out the infamous words, "I've got an idea!". Hehehehe...

Chapter 5
Coast-to-Coast

Persuading Gyula to join me on another adventure wasn't as difficult as I thought; he was quite eager to make this happen. Common sense should have told us to attempt our hike across England in the middle of the summer. Higher odds of better weather and definitely more daylight, but here we were sitting on our third train of the day travelling from Lancaster to St Bees on the 16th of March 2012. It was a slow, rickety train that progressed steadily through many small towns and villages, following the coast around the Lake District in the north east of England. Becoming immersed in some fantastic scenery on our right and the sea on our left gave me time to think. The conversation between Gyula and I had stopped an hour or so ago; partly because we had initially been chatting with excitement for four hours, but mainly because we were only minutes away from reaching our stop and the start of our next adventure. I guess the nerves, along with the reality of the task at hand, was poking us in the chest a little. I sat there feeling the cast iron wheels vibrate through the well-worn seat thinking about the friendship between me and Gyula. He had only been living in England for a few years but had strangely found his way into this relationship with me that had taken him through one disorganised adventure to another without so much as a 'maybe we should at least think about this', come out of his mouth. This poor man constantly accepted and believed I knew what I was doing, trusting me that everything would be alright. Now here we were again, sitting in what felt like a 20-year-old train, both of us with a rucksack by our side bulging with the entirety of our world for the next five days.

Hahaha, I can't believe how naive I was to think we were prepared. The rucksacks consisted of the contents of another shopping trip to the local outdoor warehouse - a £10 sleeping bag; a £10 roll mat; spare underwear; pac-a-mac waterproofs; a few spare t-shirts; a fleece; two litres of water; plenty of energy and nut bars; packets of porridge; a head torch and a small handbook titled 'Coast to Coast Path': '109 maps and guides to 31 towns and villages from St. Bees to Robin Hood's Bay'. It was this book and this book alone that I thought would be sufficient to guide us across 192 miles of English countryside, taking in the Lake District, the Yorkshire Dales and the Yorkshire Moors. Who needs an Ordnance Survey Map? Oh, and a small bottle of whisky for any emergency that might need a shot of whisky. No wonder we were starting to feel a bit trippy.

Standing up and throwing the bag onto my back as we pulled into St Bees, my legs were already made of jelly. I think they knew what was coming more than I did, and this was their last gasp attempt to change my mind, but we were now committed. We had created a little following for the challenge and had raised over £1000 for Red Nose Day during the build-up to this moment. The time was just after 11am as we stepped onto the platform to find our bearings. Looking through the trusted book, we found our direction and headed towards the coast and the starting post of the path. Within half a mile we were looking at the Irish Sea with its ripples softly brushing the pebbles of the shore. The plan was to start at exactly midday, so with half an hour to spare, we took a seat on the grass close to a signpost that read, 'Start of the Coast to Coast', and had a coffee with a nut bar.

A few moments later and in deep thought, Gyula mentioned that it was time, so in the tradition of the challenge, we had to start with our boots in the sea, and both picked up a pebble from the beach. This was to be carried in our pocket until we reached Robin Hood's Bay, hopefully less than 120 hours later where we would joyfully stand in the sea once again to release the pebble back to where it belonged - into the sea. I say hopefully, but we did actually need to finish on time. I had already booked the return journey by bus and train from Robin Hood's Bay back to Leicester, five days and four hours after our midday planned start, here at St. Bees. Apart from the train journeys to the beginning and back home at the end, I had nothing else booked. That was as far as my planning went. Buy a book, buy a sleeping bag, get some non-refundable train tickets, ask a friend to join me, and start walking.

We were off, along the beach and straight up onto the coastal path that snaked along the dominating cliffs where, if you were lucky, you could grab a glimpse of some puffins nesting on the rocks below. Continuing along you pass the first iconic checkpoint of the trek, the St. Bees Lighthouse. This is where you start heading east, inland, and physically face the peaks that lay ahead, the Lake District. Such a beautiful part of the world; it's the English countryside on steroids, and we were about to walk the fifty-plus miles over the top of it in less than a day and a half. We were buzzing, we were motoring, chatting away like a pair of garden fencers putting the world to rights. The next time we lifted our heads to take note of our progress, we'd already covered the first 13 miles, and suddenly found ourselves being overshadowed by the mountainous terrain surrounding us; then, pulled alongside Ennerdale Water for a pleasant lakeside stroll that lasted the next couple of miles. The rough plan for the day was to make it to a youth hostel called Black Sail, where I'd called a few weeks prior to see if we needed to book a bed for the night, at which time I was assured wouldn't be necessary. Leaving the southern side of the lake 17 miles into the day and approaching 5pm, we were well over halfway to the hostel, feeling well in control and ecstatic about our progress. But, knowing it was March, we also knew the sun would drop quickly and darkness would surround us by 6.30pm. With this, we stepped it up a gear and started marching towards Black Sail only 6 miles further along.

It was just shy of 7pm when we knocked on the door of our accommodation for the evening, relieved, hungry, tired, and so looking forward to a warm drink. The door opened to a flood of chat, hustle and bustle, laughter and storytelling. I could also smell hot chocolate as the opening door allowed a rush of warm air to force its way through the gap and enclose us. That, however, was as far as the pleasantries went. It took three attempts from the mouth attached to the face that was squeezed in the crack of the door to Willy Wonka's chocolate factory to tell us that the hostel was full. I refused to accept the information that was being repeatedly presented to me. All I wanted was a warm room and maybe a taste of that hot chocolate, but it wasn't to be; we weren't even allowed to spend the night on the stone floor; we had to leave.

Pitch black and with cheap head torches, temperature now steadily dropping towards freezing, hungry and worried about where we'd be able to get our head down for the night, we pushed on up the mountain trying to follow the route laid down in the book. The book only has pencilled drawings of the route. If you stray from it, you have no way of knowing where you are, especially with the reference points taken away as the darkness wrapped itself around us. It was 1:00am and we were truly panicking. Now traversing like crabs along the side of what I can only assume was the side of a very steep mountain, one head torch had given up and the other barely casting shadows, visibility had now scarily deteriorated to a few feet. We were shivering, starving, dehydrated and looking for anywhere we could bunk down for the night; anything that could give us even the slightest reprieve from the elements. At the point I couldn't take another step; my knee hit a rock sending me head over heels and onto the floor. This rock, by pure chance, was part of a small squarish windbreak for local sheep, with no roof, but it had four one-meter-tall walls and a small entrance which happened to be where I fell in. "This will have to do," I whispered into Gyula's ear as I guarded my words from the howling wind.

I don't think either of us got more than an hour's sleep. We relied on zipping both sleeping bags together for body heat, and an occasional mouth full of whisky to warm us from the inside. See, I told you that the whisky was essential! Ha-ha,

Once the new day broke, we could finally glance over the drystack stone wall to see the damage. We had quite impressively deposited ourselves on the only secure platform in view, on an extremely steep slope that continued dropping into the valley 1,000 feet below. We required a plan and quickly. After using the last of our water to make a big bowl of porridge to warm us up, we headed for the highest point we could to hopefully find a path, or maybe other people if we were lucky. Two hours later, after summiting many peaks, we heard voices which eventually turned into actual living people. We were on a path; we didn't know what path, but we didn't care; it was a path. Very dehydrated, extremely tired and, by now, starting to accept we had already been beaten on our quest, we headed in what we hoped was east until a junction of paths appeared in front of us with a few other hikers scattered around. They were extremely helpful in pointing us in the direction of Borrowdale, the next nearest village with shelter and food.

That was pretty much the last thing I remember. Apparently, twenty minutes into the descent I went to the floor, blacking out, losing all sensory connection with my surroundings. I still can't remember any of this. One minute I'm at the top talking to some fellow hikers, the next, I was lying on the tarmac at the bottom of the valley. Gyula handled the situation very professionally, quickly bringing me back to my feet. He later told me I went to the dirt six or seven more times, continuously being encouraged back to my feet. All I can vaguely remember is hearing Gyula's voice instructing me to follow his feet. Ten minutes inside my subconscious world was closer to three hours as I stumbled, crashed and tripped my way down the mountain; eventually planting my face on the asphalt at the bottom. I woke up outside a youth hostel in the back of an ambulance with a drip in my arm, and a paramedic stating how bloody stupid I was to even be out there. He carried on aggressively by saying he had better things to do with his time than to come and rescue an idiot like me, who clearly had no concept of what he was doing. Suffering from exhaustion, malnutrition and being very dehydrated, he demanded we both stay at the hostel for the night before being dropped at the local train station at the crack of dawn and sent home. Of course, we agreed. With a couple of bowls of warm soup in our bellies, we headed off to bed. The only thought I had was, how could I explain to everyone who had supported us that we didn't even make it through the first day? This question was the last and only thing I could think about as my eyes very suddenly became heavy, and I was gone.

Waking up at 4.30am staring at the springs of Gyula's bunk bed above me, the question I fell to sleep thinking about was gone. I had a couple of new ones though. Firstly, could I finish this? A day and a half into the challenge, covering only 27 miles in the first 39 hours, could I still finish this: and secondly, was there enough time? Could we do the remaining 165 miles in three and a half days? The answer, yes, we could; mathematically anyway. Then came another question - why? Why should I put myself through this? After all, I had the perfect excuse to pull out; I was in an ambulance only hours ago. Why? Because strangely, there was nothing telling me I shouldn't. Another question, did I want to carry on? Damn right I did! I couldn't tell you why I had wanted to, but I felt an energy and desire to get up and march. Maybe it was the words of the paramedic still vibrating in my ears; maybe I couldn't lose face, and maybe I didn't want to let Gyula down. I just knew it was game on. Jumping straight out of bed I woke Gyula, whispering in his ears, "we need to go". I thought there would be resistance, but he was as keen as me. Minutes later we were packed and tiptoeing down the stairs. The landlord was as adamant as the paramedic about sending us home and we didn't want that discussion at five in the morning. We made it out, onto the street and straight onto the Coast-to-Coast path, full of enthusiasm and excitement with a new bounce in our feet and chatting away again like a couple of school kids.

The original roughly planned traverse across the country had been thrown out the window. We were already 35 to 40 miles behind. We started executing a new plan, which was simple. Walk until we couldn't walk anymore; sleep, assess where we were and walk until we couldn't walk any more again, for three and a half days.

We covered 42 miles during that day, but we needed more. The terrain and the quantity of ascent and descent made for an extremely hard and a very well deserved 42 miles. Within a mile of leaving Borrowdale, we hit the bottom of the mountains where the route steeply climbed, passing various crags and Gibson's Knott before dropping into the next valley of Easedale. We found a local shop and devoured some local pasties and a couple of coffees to refuel for the next big ascent, which would eventually take us to a split in the path; a high route taking on the famous Helvellyn, or the lower, easier route circling it. The original idea was to tackle Helvellyn, but because we were chasing miles it was unfortunately the lower route. The next ten miles were stunning; I only wish we could have taken the time to enjoy the splendour of nature's canvas instead of gliding through on our mission. We remained at high altitude, passing Patterdale before descending to Haweswater Reservoir which brought the welcome relief of a flat, easy-footed path, which in turn increased our speed.

It wasn't long before the signpost welcoming us to Snap was passed, marking the end of the Lake District and into flatter farming land. Before the darkness engulfed us again, we stopped for a little bite to eat, appreciating the mountain range behind us with the utmost respect. We hit Orton and a perfect little village B&B called The George Hotel just before 10pm, where a lovely, helpful landlady welcomed us, sat us down and made us a massive bowl of soup. Booking a room, we explained we had to be out incredibly early so would unfortunately miss the breakfast. "Nonsense", she replied, "what time will you be leaving? I'll make sure you have something to eat before you go". She did just that, and it was amazing; a perfect spread; a full English with the works, coffee, tea, and orange juice. It was proudly laid out for us as we dragged ourselves into the bar at 5.30am. Shovelling every crumb and drop down, we felt almost too full to move, but it was time.

The day was quite uneventful, apart from going off track a couple of times as we passed some beautiful English countryside on our way through some authentic northern villages and small towns. At Kirkby Stephen we took our first break of the day for a coffee and a flapjack from a local tearoom. This helped us on our way across the Yorkshire Dales, past Ravenseat and Keld where we had a short nutrition break again, before overcoming Ivelet, Gunnerside, Blades, Kearton and Healaugh. It wasn't until three miles from Reeth that Gyula had his first big drop. Within minutes he went from his usual bubbly, joyful self, full of energy and enthusiasm, to a very beaten and broken man. He struggled to even lift his feet onto a four-inch-high roadside curb, instead, choosing to slide up the driveway recess of the next house, his left leg dragging behind him as if it had a mind of its own and refused to play with him anymore. Nearly in tears, he persuaded me we couldn't make it to our intended destination that night, which was Richmond, a further ten miles ahead. Instead, we found a B&B in Reeth to settle down. Making it to Richmond would have given us 48 miles for the day and 74 miles left for Robin Hood's Bay. But with only 37 miles completed that day and a total of only 108 miles achieved in the first three and a half days, the end was really starting to look too much.

Once again, settling down to a huge bowl of soup (it seems all they ate around there was thick, loaded soup and crusty bread), late into the evening and chatting to another very sympathetic landlady at a B&B called Hilary House, Gyula emphatically gazed at me declaring it was game over for him. He had made the difficult decision to find his way home in the morning. Richmond was the biggest town in the area, and if we were to quit and go home, Richmond would be the place to do it from. This wasn't an option for me. I had already made the decision back in the hostel two days ago that I was going to finish this. It wasn't a wish, it wasn't a hope, and it wasn't a maybe. Regardless of anything or anyone's influence, I was going to finish this. The determination and single-mindedness hadn't faltered from waking up in the bunk bed. There was no other priority in my world. I was being driven by a pure survival instinct to finish. It had nothing to do with family, pride, charity or promise. Every cell and thought process was taking me towards the only goal that existed. I tried to explain this to Gyula as he lifted his bum onto the next step of the staircase, reversing his way up to our room because his legs wouldn't work. He understood and asked me to wake him up before I left at silly o'clock in the morning to wish me well.

My alarm vibrated just once before I bolted out of bed as if it were Christmas morning, fell into my clothes, made an extremely dark cup of coffee before nudging Gyula. "See you later brother. I hope you have a safe trip home and give everyone a hug from me". As I crept out of the room, Gyula whispered after me, "You really doing this?" "Definitely", I replied." You're a bloody idiot!" he responded, "Just fucking wait, I'm coming"; and with that, the game was on again. We had 84 miles left and 30 hours in which to do it, and we still had the joys of the Yorkshire Moors to deal with!

It was time to be smart, ha-ha, when have I ever been smart? Spreading everything we had onto the bed, we decided to leave anything behind we didn't need for the next 30 hours. Sleeping bags, sleeping mats, extra clothing; even some of the energy bars and glucose tablets. All we took was some food, water, waterproofs and a spare fleece. Let's do this!

After navigating the stairs on our backsides, we left a thank-you note to the landlady and headed out into the darkness. For the first mile or so we didn't have joints in our knees, but they soon gave up and we began striding as if we were extras in 'Dad's Army'; heads down, with only one intention - getting home. Richmond came upon us just in time for Harvey's Cafe to open, and we devoured the largest breakfast they had to offer.

With a belly full of processed protein and our blood full of caffeine, the mission became the focus once again. Marching on past woodlands, moors, farmers' fields, and roadways, undulating hills and then flatlands, with music in our ears, we scarcely spoke. Lost in separate worlds but fixated on the same quest. Our heads didn't lift until reality returned in the form of a soldier marching in the opposite direction, fully loaded with his tactical rucksack ladening his back. Hours had passed whilst we'd been lost in our subconscious state, so we were glad to stop and share a few stories with the squaddie. He was also hiking the Coast to Coast, obviously in the opposite direction, and coincidentally had started around the same time as us, approximately four days ago. However, he did feel a little upset and looked at us in disbelief when we mentioned this statistic. He had covered 58 miles in four days whereas we had more than doubled this with 134 miles in the bag. He really didn't like this, but with the obligatory man hugs and well-wishing, we moved on. Another 20 minutes down the path we hit the A167 dual carriageway with a service station conveniently placed by its side. Lunchtime! 55 miles to the sea and it was 4pm. We had 20 hours of the five days left. We loaded up the backpacks with food, water and cold coffee and headed for the hills, again...well the Yorkshire Moors. Accepting this was going to be an extremely difficult night, having already accumulated 29 miles, the conversation lifted our spirits, along with the notion we had outperformed the military man thus far.

It was another three hours before we hit the first of three ascents that was a sign, we were about to start crossing the Yorkshire Moors. The soldier had pre-warned us earlier about these three peaks. At the top of the third ascent, the moors would spread out in front of us for 19 miles before returning down to civilisation. The Yorkshire Moors' shelf sits around 400 metres above sea level (1400 feet) and although that's not too much of an altitude, it did further bring the mercury down. I'm not exactly sure of the temperature, but the ground was crispy as we planted our feet one step at a time nearer to the chequered flag, and we perfectly imitated steam trains with our rhythmic exhalations into the soft light of our head torches. Wrapped up in only a couple of t-shirts, a windproof jacket and fleece hat, it wasn't long before the uncontrollable shaking took hold, informing us that hyperthermia could be the next issue if we weren't careful.

It was well past midnight when we crested the third ascent onto the Moors. Already asking for more from our blistered, swollen feet, and mentally scraping the bottom of the barrel for anything that could give us even a minute of escapism from this tortuous situation, seconds passed in slow motion. Every mile was a half marathon slog, with the only witnesses to our despair being the occasional demonic gazes from the grazing sheep, sporadically dotted around the blanket of the blinding darkness. The miles and hours started taking hold of Gyula by around two or three in the morning when I could see him desperately losing the fight, insisting he had to sleep. "Just for a couple of hours", he pleaded. Then the frequency of his persuasions increased, as he asked for an hour: "Please, Stu", he carried on, "just an hour". Then 20 minutes, "Just give me 20 minutes" he begged. His voice became more agitated and aggressive as I repeatedly assured him that, in these conditions, in our physical state, and in these clothes, we probably wouldn't wake up; we must carry on. This only infuriated him further, eventually igniting a huge argument in the middle of the Moors in the pitch black, and with only sheep as referees. Gyula is a very tolerant man who never gets worked up. In fact, this is still the only time I have ever seen him blow in 15 years. His last remark before storming off into the opaqueness was him affirming that he didn't want to see me again for at least six months once we'd returned home, and sharing, very sternly, that he would never join me on any ridiculous challenge or adventure again. I am a stupid, incompetent and dangerously underprepared idiot, he carried on, and I had put both our lives in danger... He was right, of course.

The next couple of hours we followed the path as it wound its way across the Moors, past The Lion Inn and down into Glaisdale. We were separated by 50 metres of dense, impenetrable airspace as we both listened to our music whilst going through a barrage of emotions.

My most powerful ally is LOVE; the love for my wife and the love for my children. Just missing them and feeling I was letting them down was enough to carry me through any situation. When Myia was born and we carried her out of the hospital, placing her delicately but securely into the baby chair of the car and starting the engine, the song on the radio was 'Hero' by Enrique Inglesius. That's all I ever wanted to be for my children - a hero. That song has always been a strength for me, which is why I had it on a continuous loop for two hours as I cried my way out of the darkness and the Moors, to arrive outside a newsagent in the centre of Glaisdale just as it opened at 6am.

That was one of the hardest nights I've ever experienced; crossing the whole of the Yorkshire Moors in darkness, totally underprepared, angry with the only other human being in my present world, and now totally exhausted after having already covered 63 miles.

That newsagent was a godsend. Still ignoring each other, we fell into the shop, grabbed as much food as we could carry, then perched ourselves at opposite ends of a bench on the other side of the road. By the time we had licked the last calorie from our fingers, the tension between us had gone. We apologised, hugged each other and got back to the job at hand. Nineteen miles to go with five and a half hours left. A big ask, as our legs were shot. Once again, our knees and ankles were so inflamed, they refused to give mobility, but 'hey ho', we'd have to walk from the hips; it was pointless dwelling on it. It was time to go home. The first mile took over half an hour, the second 25 minutes; each one getting quicker as we passed village after village, walking along main roads and through wooded areas. Honestly, I can't remember any of it. All I could see was the four feet in front of me. With five miles left and 75 minutes remaining on the clock, we had a chance - we might actually pull this off. Then, in a blink of an eye, Gyula stopped...he just stopped! Mentally and physically, everything in him shouted NO! NO MORE! It didn't matter what I said or did to encourage him, he was finished. In the end, days later, he told me, that it was just understanding there was no recovery or back-up support that made him once again shuffle forward. It was the realisation that there was no plan B. If he was to make it home, he had to get to the end; if he wanted the pain to stop; if he wanted to feel the cuddle from his loved ones, then he had to get to the end. Every emotion he had; his love, his anger, his pride, his resentment, his fear and his sadness, all needed to come together to encourage his limbs to take another step. It was hard to witness, my brother dragging each foot in turn, balancing most of his body weight on the bending walking poles. I could have run those last five miles, I felt just as pumped and driven as I was when I leapt out of bed in the hostel three and half days ago, but Gyula couldn't even lift his head to shout at me. I wasn't angry or disappointed; I was supportive, empathetic and proud. I have never seen someone give so much of themselves to a cause before, or since. I believe it was this moment, in this situation, sharing this pain and discomfort, that I knew we would grow old with each other, sharing many other, not-so-hazardous adventures together. With only a couple of miles left we reached the coastal path, which would take us to the chequered flag. Seeing, smelling, hearing and tasting the sea in the air lifted both our spirits, and the pace increased slightly. Robin Hood's Bay is a small holiday town at the bottom of a very steep road. We were bumping off every pole, dustbin, streetlight and barrier as we passed all the tourists, looking like we had been lost in the wild for a month. Eventually descending into the water and letting the North Sea caress our dusty boots, we stared through each other, took the pebbles from our pockets and threw them as far as we could. Sounds dramatic, but probably looked quite pathetic as they only travelled a few feet. We had no strength left and both our backs were locked. "Fancy a pint?" "Yep", Gyula replied. Tradition states that, after completion, you must go into the Bay Hotel, 30 feet from where we stood, for a drink and to mark your accomplishment in the leather-bound book placed in the entrance. Best-tasting pint I have ever had!

The journey home had its own challenges, made worse by making the mistake of removing our boots halfway down the pint. I visually noticed my feet increase in size as they tasted freedom, and then refusing to allow me to put them back on. I couldn't get shoes on my feet for a week afterwards. We needed to catch a bus to Scarborough, which of course had to be at the top of the Bay. From there we had to jump on our first train, but before we did, we visited a fast-food restaurant. This train took us to Sheffield for a connecting train to Leicester, so whilst waiting at Sheffield we visited another fast-food restaurant. Arriving in Leicester, we grabbed more food before departing the station and into the arms of our loved ones. All this was done barefoot. I can't remember expressing much of the joy I felt inside. I owed Teri more, but 40 hours of consciousness and 84 miles in the legs left an empty shell for Teri to, once again, nurture back to a human being.

It took a couple of days before emotions returned, tears flowed, and I was able to share even the smallest of stories with my family. Trying to explain how I had felt a drive and focus I'd never experienced before, and how I loved it and just wanted to feel it again. But the more I spoke, the more confused they looked.

Gyula also stuck to his word and has never accompanied me on any further adventures. He is still the best friend anyone could wish for, but he has gone his own way regarding exercise and challenges.

Now I was on my own and in need of a bigger fix once again, so I looked around for something bigger, something outside of the UK. This is what led, firstly to the Black Ice Race, and then to the 2013 edition of the 6633 Arctic Ultra.

Part 2
The Development Years

Chapter 6
Melvin

Two weeks after returning home from the Coast-to-Coast and feeling physically recovered, I often found myself waking up at silly o'clock in the morning, staring at the dark shadows on the artexed ceiling of our bedroom that were cast by the streetlamp that persuaded its soft light through the curtains. I spent hours contemplating how I had changed during those few days. I now felt different; I felt taller; I felt awakened; I felt self-belief. I felt I had just been given the right of passage, and the freedom to not just ask for whatever I wanted, but to claim it. For my first 38 years my parents, aunties, uncles, grandparents, teachers and bosses had been telling me I had no belief in myself; that I was capable of more; I just needed confidence in my own abilities.

I honestly felt I had been progressing during those years, listening to these older, wiser voices and using their advice to build a more confident, resilient and driven version of myself that had the strength to overcome any of life's little bumps or intimidating mountains that may obstruct me. Maybe I had, to a certain degree, but I had no idea how powerful the human spirit could be until I had felt and overcome fear.

Now, I'm not talking about the fear of going to the dentist, going into an exam, sitting your driving test or going on a first date. I am talking about the fear of maybe not making it home...ever again; maybe not seeing your children...ever again.

I know and understand that I was only walking across this nice safe country of England, and help could always be reached if needed. I'm not trying to over-dramatise the achievement. I understand I was never really in any true life-threatening situation like evacuating my family from a war zone, or crossing the Arctic, or sitting beside your child in a hospital bed not knowing if they would wake up. Compared to that, this was like a challenging holiday, but it was the first time in my life I had overcome my own fear. It was the first time in my life I had wholeheartedly stood straight up after being beaten to the floor, knowing that failure, and every thought process related to a possible outcome of failure, had been eliminated. It was the first time that I KNEW I was going to be successful way before the conclusion arrived. Obstacles in my way were irrelevant. The negative, internal voices were silenced, fear of failure was gone, and disappointment, physical damage or strangely, even death wasn't an option. Even any thought of getting home to see Teri and the girls took a back seat. I had one target and one target only: the successful completion of the task at hand. Nothing else mattered. The power came from knowing it was already a foregone conclusion. It didn't matter what stood in front of me; I was capable and would walk straight through it. This is what I mean by overcoming the fear of what's in front of me.

For the first time, I felt how absolute Melvin was; how indisputable the human spirit can be when placed into a situation the rational thinking brain cannot compute on its own.

Melvin is the name I give the monkey who is perched on my right shoulder that whispers into my ear when it wants an indulgence like a croissant, a cake, a bar of chocolate or a pint. He also whispers into my ear when he doesn't want to do something like go to the gym, finish a race or stand up in the face of adversity. Basically, he wants all the joyful and pleasurable experiences in life without suffering any of the pain or discomfort this world can give us, regardless of whether it's good for me or not. Melvin doesn't understand consequence; he lives purely for the present. He doesn't understand that eight pints of beer can ruin my weekend, and continuous abuse of the stuff could result in liver disease. He only knows that it feels amazing right now. He doesn't understand that 20 cigarettes a day may result in lung cancer. He only knows that on 20 separate occasions today I had five minutes to myself, allowing me to relax away from the kids, the boss or my life, and it felt great. He also understands that staying away from the gym or from that early morning walk I promised myself feels a lot more pleasant than the sweat, muscle ache and fatigue that comes with doing the right thing. But he's not aware that thirty years of a sedentary lifestyle will encourage a whole host of illnesses that could kill me prematurely. Melvin is the second voice in my head that I'm constantly arguing with. But on occasion, when the shit really hits the fan, when there is no room for alternatives, the two voices in my head stop arguing about whether this is a good idea or not and, instead, rally together to beat a common enemy. This is when the magic happens; this is when you start to discover what you are capable of and what you need to do to survive. I felt that authentic emotion for the first time on this trek. The same emotion that our cave-dwelling ancestors used and relied upon day after day in order to make it to the end of the day in one piece; and I liked it. This was before we evolved and felt our need to rationalise everything, creating disruption throughout our thought processes. I was instantly addicted to its purity. With no need to worry about the mortgage, work, days of the week and balancing any of life's commitments, the emotional connection to just the present, and surviving it, was overwhelmingly definitive. I had to have more. I had to feel that way again.

Lying there staring at the Himalayan peaks and troughs of the artexed ceiling, I knew everything had changed; I had changed. I had thought I knew who I was, what I was capable of, where I was heading and what my future entailed, but I was wrong. Only weeks before, my book, my story, was already written and I was moseying through the pages, taking on one chapter at a time to the inevitable last page. Now I understood I was able to write each page as I went, and as it developed.

So, what do I want to write about in my book? What kind of story do I want it to be? The decision was suddenly mine; well, it always had been if I'm honest; I just chose to accept things before, for what they were.

From this point, things started changing. It wasn't a conscious move in any direction; I just knew things weren't the way they were supposed to be. Teri wasn't supposed to be in a wheelchair; I wasn't supposed to be sitting in an office being dictated to and waiting for the praise to come in my direction during my next review. My girls weren't supposed to start their lives stepping over a drunken dad lying halfway up the stairs, and we weren't supposed to be living a life where every page and every chapter was predetermined.

This is how I see the predetermined book that has been written for us in the first world:

First chapter: EDUCATION - learn what a successful human being is. Through a collection of well-selected subjects and programmes you will learn how to progress into adulthood. This includes infant school, primary, junior and high school as a bare minimum, then hopefully onto college and/or university. All of them slowly sowing the seeds and giving you what you need to achieve a pre-set life. Showing you how you should behave and conduct yourself to be categorised as a successful and contributing human.

Second chapter: MARRY - Make more little people, which I have to say is very enjoyable. But don't worry if you're not sure how to educate your children because there are plenty of ways to support and raise your children for you, so you can concentrate on the next chapter.

Third chapter: EARN MONEY - The more money you earn, the better. This is so you can buy and build a life full of materialistic necessities that have been dictated to you in previous teachings so you can be identified as that successful human, i.e., the four-bedroom, detached house with a twin garage. BMWs on the drive; big TVs; two holidays a year, one in the snow and one in the sun; a family Labrador; a hefty pension; meals out; expensive designer clothes; exquisite jewellery and all the other signs of success.

Fourth chapter: KNOWLEDGE - Make sure you pass this preached knowledge onto your loved ones and direct them onto the same path.

Fifth chapter: ENJOY RETIREMENT - When you've given nearly fifty years to the book and built a successful life, full of comforts, toys, gadgets and possessions, it's time to sit back and relish in all your accolades. You've earned it, after all. You have the weathered, broken, dysfunctional body and mind to prove it.

NOOOO! No more! I'm not doing this anymore! I wasn't sure what I was supposed to be doing or where it was taking me, but let's roll the dice. First job first, I thought. We needed to be healthy, all of us. I couldn't, and we couldn't as a family, be ready for whatever came next if we didn't have the energy, fitness, enthusiasm and capabilities to run with our new life when it arrived. This is when I started reading. Book after book would pass my eyes in my unrelenting thirst to be better. How many times as a child did you hear someone quote "knowledge is power"? As a child, you very quickly brush over it, thinking it's just a ploy to get you to do your homework, but at the age of 39 years old I understood. I was getting more powerful by the day. Using this power, we began making our house a healthier one, and our dreams of what could be possible ran away with us.

You see, health is the foundation that makes everything possible, and I mean everything. In the 'house of my life' (pinched this from Karl), health is the actual foundation that holds the house up; and just like in any house, if the foundations are weak, the house will eventually crumble. Equally, if the construction of the ground floor isn't built strongly enough to hold the rest up, it will collapse into itself. Lastly, you need a sturdy first floor to hold the roof up. So, with this knowledge, I had to decide what materials I would use to build the rest of my house. There are two choices: one for the ground floor and one for the first floor. One of these choices is LOVE and the other is MISSION. There's no right or wrong when it comes to which way around I could choose; I just had to make sure that the strongest for me personally is on the ground floor, as this needs to hold up the rest of the house. For me, without question, its LOVE. The love for my world is the reason I get up early every morning. It's the reason I continue to strive for growth; it's the reason I accept discomforts and pain in my life with open arms to make sure my loved ones don't have to. My MISSION, therefore, finds its place on the first floor. This is my need to educate, teach, help and motivate people; to encourage them to work and thrive for more; to enrich them. This is why I have my health club and why I am writing this book. The decision of what to place on my ground floor and my first floor is mine and personal to me; it's not the same for everyone. I would imagine the Elon Musks, Alan Sugars, Duncan Banatynes and Richard Bransons of this world would have their MISSION as the ground floor and LOVE on the first. I would imagine that to be as successful as they are, their missions would be the thing they wake up and go to sleep thinking about. It's what excites them and drives them. It doesn't mean they don't absolutely love immensely the people they cuddle up to in the evening, but their passion to be successful is very powerful.

Lastly, to finish the house of my life, I would need to fill the roof. This space is for all the stuff: the cars, the holidays, the nice clothes, the meals out, the gym membership, the Sky subscription, and the pleasantries. The nice things that make life more enjoyable; the materialistic things that are preached to us from an early age, and that make us believe they are the signs of a successful person.

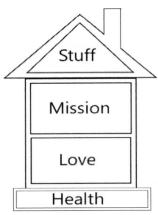

And ending up with something that looks like this:

As you can see, HEALTH is the foundation that holds everything up. If you want a better relationship with your partner, you better make sure you are healthy enough to have the energy to give them the time they deserve after your shift is done. When you arrive home after a measly eight to ten hours at work, how are you going to show your partner the love they want or the help they need around the house if tiredness arrives prematurely? How are you going to devote that irreplaceable time with your children that is required to raise them happily, healthily and full of ambition and respect, if you fall asleep every night as they tug on your trouser leg for attention?

I came to realise that my relationships need quality time to survive and grow; otherwise, my marriage will collapse, my children will fail, and friendships will dwindle. Being a successful colleague, boss, educator and supporter all need my energy. If I didn't look after my own and my family's health first, the supporting ground floor will crumble. Think about it: how important is progressing on your mission and the need to be successful, after you've had an argument with a loved one? How important is the new car or the planned family holiday when someone in your world isn't talking to you because of a nasty row? This happened very frequently to me in my past. I have been too quick off the mark in recent years at blaming everyone else for the wrongdoings in my life. Maybe I just wasn't physically or mentally healthy enough to cope with the difficult situations. Because I was unhealthy, tired and fatigued, it was easier to blame someone or something else for my inadequacies.

Realising that my love and relationships held an especially important supporting role in my life, I could progress further up the construction of my house. I now understood that sufficient energy for my relationships was needed to create a ground floor solidly built on top of the foundation of health; then I would have the drive and enthusiasm to work on my MISSION.

Ask yourself the same questions I asked myself. What do you actually want? What do you want to achieve? Do you want a better position in the business? Do you want your own business? Do you want more free time by earning the same amount in a shorter space of time? Do you want a career change? Do you want to move? Do you just want to earn more money? Do you want the freedom to pursue personal goals? Do you want to travel or to educate? Whatever you or I want, unless you are healthy enough and have the energy needed to work the extra hours, put in the overtime, to be enthusiastic enough to learn a new skill after your shift, to make yourself more valuable and freeing up time, you can't and won't manage it without health and the support of your loved ones. Short term, most of us can battle through difficult or demanding times, but the lack of health will eventually show through, and failure is inevitable. This is why my career moved and grew very quickly once I knew how to build my house. I went from an unhappy truck driver to owning a successful health club within a few years. Once I was healthy and I gave the attention and love to my loved ones, which was lacking before, my mission became so much easier to grow and manipulate. I had the energy and encouragement to roll with the punches and react positively to any situation. See how it works?

Time to put the roof on. Spending time every day making better dietary choices, keeping hydrated, exercising, obtaining adequate rest, recouping time and spending time outside, will build a healthy and active mind and body. This will enable me to give 100% of myself to the people around me, which will be echoed back, filling my heart with the love we all crave. This fulfilment will spark the creative nature within, helping me to strive to be the best version of myself in order to work on my mission. Then, and only then, will I have a house that really appreciates the little luxuries in life that the modern world can provide, and I can fill my roof with them.

Here's the problem as I see it. Most of our houses in the first world (as we've labelled it) are upside down. We are

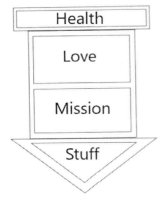

balancing our entire 'house of my life' on the small fragile point of the roof, expecting it to be strong and supportive enough to encourage a happy life. We rely on the small, insignificant achievements of purchasing stuff to satisfy the 'instant gratification' enviro-nment we have become accustomed to.

This inevitably leads to debt that then eventually progresses into a necessity to work more hours in a job we don't truly like, instead of working on our mission. I've spent too many hours performing miserably in a position I couldn't stand, only to return home and take it out on my wife and daughters, which then destroys the LOVE part of my house of health. With no more financial credit to be given, overtime swallowing up all my spare time and my closest loved ones dysfunctional and crying out for attention, the thought of being healthy is the last thing on the mind.

So, as mentioned right at the beginning of this chapter, first things first. It was time to work on our health and rebuild the house from the foundations up.

Another awakening from the stroll across the country was how powerful and influential other people's energy can be. It's very subtle, but unquestionably noticeable how a mood can be changed by the presence of a new person within earshot. You can be in a perfect, upbeat, bouncy mood, then feel anger within minutes from being emotionally downloaded on.

When I literally had nothing left to give, collapsing at the top of the mountain the morning after that difficult first night sleeping in the sheep enclosure, I realised it was Gyula's energy that continually got me back on my feet. Time after time his energy and spirit demanded I make it back down for help. It was also Gyula's *lack* of energy traversing the Yorkshire Moors through the night that increased the difficulty of the situation to near breaking point, thus creating an argument and a negative environment. I know that sounds harsh; after all, we were both equally distraught and took it out on each other, but it's an example we can relate to.

This reminded me of something I had heard at a Mother Nature's Diet seminar years before but didn't really pay any attention to at the time. Things were now different. Now I had felt first-hand how demanding other people's moods could be on my own. I now understood; I now got it and began using this next tool I'm about to show you. I used it to build security around my newly discovered devotion to life and my newly-built 'House of my Life'.

So, I started by drawing a triangle and pointing it towards the top of the page, like a pyramid. I then divided it from the bottom to the point equally into four separate sections.

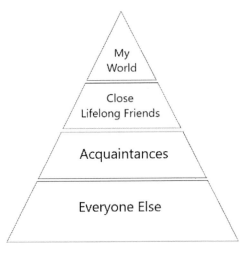

These four sections are where every person on the planet lives within my world.

In the small triangle at the very top of the pyramid is where my deepest-loved people live: Teri, Myia and Keira.

The next section down is for the people in my life I would class as close friends. The people whom I could count on at any time of the day or night, and the people I would happily change my day for, without question or hesitation. These could be family, or even friends that you would class as family, remembering - and this sounds harsh - blood doesn't necessarily mean you are close. I can say at this stage of my journey there are less than twenty people who live in this section.

The penultimate section is filled with all your acquaintances. Everyone you know; drinking buddies, golfing buddies, work colleagues, people in the street you wave to on the way to work: friends from school, recognisable faces from the gym or restaurant you've been nodding to for the last year - anyone that has a connection to your world, no matter how small.

The ground floor belongs to every other soul on the planet - the remaining six plus billion people wandering around this rock. Now, with everyone on the planet placed somewhere in your pyramid, you receive the news that everyone dreads from the doctor; the news that changes everyone's plans and re-prioritises what's important in life. You are told you have 365 days left to live: just one year, before it's all over. One year to get the best from life.

Now this is where the difficult decisions need to be made; or maybe it's not so difficult. It wasn't for me. You need to decide how many of your last 365 days you would give to each level. With only 365 days left, would you give any to the ground floor, the six plus billion unknowns in your life? That's an easy one that would be a NO from me. Would you give any to the second level? I'm afraid that would be another no from me, which I will explain more about shortly. Now to the emotionally connected people; the people in your world that make you feel good about yourself; the people you would jump out of bed at three in the morning for. Would you give any of your last 365 days to them? This is a hard decision, and this takes a little more time.

Personally, I would love to spend a couple of weeks at least with my close friends/family, maybe even a bit more. Let's keep the maths easy and say 40 days. That leaves 325 days, which I would have no regrets about spending with my world, the three people who make me who I am. Now here's the clincher; this is the reality of the situation. This is what I thought about when I was looking for strength as I fought through the darkness on the moors with Gyula 50 paces in front of me after we'd argued about not being able to sleep. One day you WILL only have 365 days left, and you have no idea what day that will be. It could be today, it could be September 22nd, 2032, or it could be 40 years from now; we just don't know. So why don't we live as if we only have 365 days left now? Answer, because we still have to live. We still need to grow; we still need to progress; we still have to enjoy and meet new people; we still need to teach and educate; we still need to help the vulnerable and less privileged, and we still need to plan for the future.

So, what's the answer? How do we find balance and make sure the right people are getting our time in the most productive way? A line has to be drawn through the middle of the pyramid. This is where I have learned to be quite harsh and selfish. The deal is, DON'T spend any of your last 365 days of existence with people who are below that line, UNLESS it benefits your quality of life with people above it. If the people below help you mentally, physically, inspirationally, emotionally, financially, or any other 'ally', then keep them around and enjoy your time with them. If they don't benefit you in any way, then I guarantee you're the one they are relying on for energy. You are the one others are using to improve their time with the people they have placed above the line. You are being used, and you are giving up valuable seconds, hours and days that cannot be retrieved. That does not mean, in any way, that you shouldn't help out your community or spend time or money with a charity you have a passionate connection with: far from it. I totally understand how much joy, fulfilment and warmth you can feel when improving someone else's day, week or life. By contributing to the improvement of someone else's life and being a part of these heart-felt tasks, breeds a unique satisfaction that can only help you enjoy, relax and feel great about yourself, allowing you to achieve better quality time with the people above the line.

With this newly downloaded information, I had to let go of the acquaintances in my life that were dragging me down and holding me back; the naysayers, the energy zappers and the green monsters; then only surround

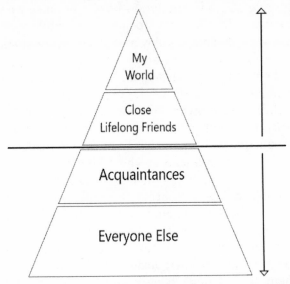

myself with people with whom I could develop alongside, learn from and create friendships. These new friendships could then, hopefully, encourage higher numbers to appear above the line. Isn't that what it's all about; spending time with people who make you feel good about yourself, life, and the world around you?

Over the next few years, with the construction of my 'House of my Life' standing on stronger foundations, and with the correct people around me, some magnificent changes started developing. Unbelievably, my wife improved, becoming more abled than disabled. I became more focused, determined and confident, believing I could change my future; which I did. This helped financially because you'll always be more successful at something you are passionate about, rather than something you just put up with. I removed a lot of the negativity and negative influences from my surroundings that had spent too much unwelcome time invading my senses, leaving space for more like-minded individuals and positive energy to fill the gap. This was a key factor when building a community of people around me that supported the cause and helped me through my own family's development, who were there to encourage and inspire me as much as I was for them.

Now looking back, I realise it was because of the accomplishment of the Coast to Coast, and the persistence through the difficulty of it, that allowed me to see Melvin as an ally for the first time. That cheeky monkey on my shoulder that constantly moans and whispers naughty stuff in my ear, also has unrelenting strength when called upon. That monkey isn't just the reason I want to eat cake and still crave a beer after eight years of being sober, but he was responsible for giving me the drive and the strength to march across the country, starting the chain of events that has led me to be sitting here, typing this book, in a lovely home with a healthy family; my life turned around, and an exciting future ahead of me.

Chapter 7
The Importance of Failure

Why is failure important? It's the point at which growth, adaptation, progression and evolution start!

We wouldn't be here, on this planet, if it weren't for our ability to learn from failure. We wouldn't have evolved from our microscopic first ancestors that lived 540 million years ago and were a bag-like creature with a huge mouth, no anus, and moved by wiggling, if we didn't learn from our genetic failings.

A human being commonly is said to have 27,000 genes. Half of each one comes from your father and half from your mother. If these 27,000 genes from one parent perfectly connect with the other 27,000 from your other parent, then you would become an exact replica of the combination of your mother and father. Fortunately, in the creation of every human, or any other living species for that matter, some of these don't quite connect, they fail. This failure could account for an endless number of variances in your development. Maybe you have one blue eye and one brown eye. It could mean you have a slightly extended spine. It could mean you are deaf in your left ear or have a leg half an inch longer than the other. The resulting scenario of one or a multiple of missed connections or genetic failures could prove to either be advantageous to your survival, or a possible disadvantage.

As mentioned, your genetic slip might have given you a longer spine. The ability to stand higher than others would be an amazing advantage when stalking prey through the tall grass, giving you the advantage of a few seconds head start when chasing down the wild hog. Having this genetic advantage means you would always be at the forefront of successful hunts, supporting your place in the tribe as the dominant hunter, and therefore creating a bit of a stir with the opposite sex and a higher chance of passing on your genes. Not to mention the convenience of gaining a few feet on others around you when the local sabre tooth tiger makes an appearance. If you survive longer, you pass on your genes more often.

What if one of the misalignments in the 27,000 genes created a hearing deficiency in your left ear? Could this result in your demise? Missing a shout from a tribal member, warning you about a falling tree or a mudslide or that bloody sabre tooth tiger, could mean the end of your genetic line? If a failure in the 27,000 connections between two gene pools during procreation created a modification, and that modification lasted at least three further generations, then it could be said that the genetic accident could be regarded as an advantageous failure, because you and the next few generations didn't die. Therefore, this new modification becomes the norm, part of the new jigsaw that makes your family's genetic code. This is the black and white of evolution. Without failure we do not adapt, and we do not evolve.

Sometimes an adaptation happens when the stresses against it are too strong, either physically or emotionally. This creates a small failure. This failure will then repair, creating a very slight variation which will hopefully allow the same applied stress more acceptable the next time it's felt.

An example of physical failure would be using a specific muscle or group of muscles in the gym until they fail - this will damage muscle fibres. These damaged fibres will repair, but they'll repair with an adaptation. This resulting adaptation may be a larger muscle, a more powerful muscle, a more responsive muscle or a more endurable muscle. Thus, creating the capability to lift more, perform more repetitions, or last longer on the next visit. When sprinting flat-out across a field, or pumping uncontrollably on a spinning bike, your ability to breathe effectively is gone, creating an uncomfortable state of panic as your lungs damage and burn under the excess load required from them. This once again forces a change whilst repairing - the forced change to this failure will be a minutely larger lung capacity with more alveoli and a more efficient gaseous exchange. This will inevitably, over time, allow you to run faster and stronger than you could before. If you recently acquired a new position at the company you work for, and this new position continually required you to carry large heavy objects, creating stiff joints, aching bones and painful muscles, eventually an adaptation would occur. The tendons and ligaments, your connective tissues around your joints, would become stronger, your muscles would evolve, and you would become more comfortable withstanding the required workload forced on your body.

What's more, your bones would increase in density allowing more pressure to be forced on them. In time, no more aches or pains whilst performing the same workload as before.

Psychologically, a similar adaptation occurs when failure is felt. For example, imagine you had the perfect childhood full of love, encouragement and guidance, and you lived in a Disney-esq village where everyone knew your name and looked out for you. Upon reaching 18, you fall into your dream job with an amazing team who provide a special friendship group and social network. This friendship group then provides the prince or princess of your life who completes your jigsaw. Between you, you build a sublime life together, full of little humans and a picture postcard cottage. With all that joy and happiness during the first half of your journey, do you think you would have developed the resilience, the fortitude, the grit and the tenacity to continue moving forward when the shit hit the fan? How would you cope when you lost your job through redundancy? How would you cope when one of your little humans became dangerously ill, or how would you be able to carry on with your daily duties during the weeks or months ahead if your cherished golden Labrador died? You wouldn't! The ability to build mental strength, grow a hard shell and develop the resilience to keep moving forward, comes from being broken; just the same as your muscles need to be broken to become stronger. You need to feel discomfort; you need to be hurt and you need to have been beaten to your knees on occasion. You must feel this before you know how to stand back up. It's the individuals who have been fighting from the ground up all their lives that fight the hardest. The more frequently they are beaten down, the more capable they are at bouncing back. To achieve this resilience, there had to be something that broke them, something that they failed at initially before overcoming it. The earlier in life this vital grit and tenacity is developed, the happier, the more comfortable and the more balanced life will be.

One of my biggest concerns as we move forward into a world where everyone is equal and everyone can be a winner, is the inability to feel loss; the inability to fail and the unwillingness to let ourselves, or anyone around us, feel any discomfort. From a very early age we are now protected and wrapped in cotton wool. We are not even allowed to use the word "fail" at school. We all receive a medal on sports day. We are continually told to wrap up, stop playing in the mud, stop climbing the tree, stop swinging across the stream, stop play fighting, stop being adventurous - stop, stop, stop! STOP LEARNING HOW TO FAIL. Failing is the biggest lesson any of us will learn throughout our life, and we now live in a world where failure is being taken away because we might feel offended or disrespected or embarrassed. I guarantee that learning how to fail as an infant is far easier than learning how to fail as an adult.

Food for thought: the highest suicide category throughout the first world is now young adults. This is the age they all realise life isn't the bed of roses they were led to believe, and you are not just entitled to the comforts in life but the discomforts too. A degree-level education doesn't automatically mean you will be comfortably wealthy, and that wealth doesn't automatically mean you are going to be happy. We have unintentionally created a generation of young adults that believe happiness exists when you reach the top of the mountain, but now we have the technology to place these young adults straight on top of the mountain making them temporarily and artificially happy. Only then do they discover that they have missed out on a vital part of the process, which is the climb. The climb is where possible and necessary failure exists. This is where there is every possibility that the top of the mountain might not even be a certainty; they might not actually get there. It's in this unknown where life happens and where happiness exists. It's the journey of successes and failures that instant gratification, unfortunately, takes away and, ultimately, a dissatisfied existence grows.

There is a difference between a physiological and a psychological failure. Most physiological failures come from you teaching your physical self a lesson, in other words, you are in control of the lesson, you decide how much resistance you force on yourself; whereas most psychological failures come from your mental self, teaching your subconscious a lesson, or you could say, you are the student being taught a lesson building resilience. Whether you choose to listen - well, that's the question.

Other times an adaptation might occur by necessity. Lighter skin became necessary as humans migrated towards the poles where the temperature is cooler and the distance from the sun farther away. In cave-dwelling times, darker skin would have been beneficial when living around the equator, to protect from the sun's strength, whilst still metabolising absorbable vitamin D. Once human settlements progressed north, past Rome or Paris, the strength of the sun wasn't powerful enough to penetrate the thicker, darker skin, resulting in lower levels of vitamin D. Vitamin D helps regulate the amount of calcium and phosphate in the body. Low levels of vitamin D leads to low levels of calcium, which in turn can encourage skeletal issues like rickets in children and osteoporosis in adults. Phosphate is three-quarters of ATP (Adenosine Triphosphate), which is the main energy currency of each and every cell in your body. ATP is your spark of energy; without sufficient phosphate, energy levels are low. The genetic slip which created a child with slightly lighter skin, who was also a member of the migrating community travelling north, could continue absorbing sufficient Vitamin D and was therefore stronger, fitter and healthier than the darker skin members. This advantage would provide this young adult more of an opportunity to procreate, becoming a mother or father, passing on the lighter gene into future generations and allowing them to migrate farther north without the loss of Vitamin D, calcium and phosphate production.

Sometimes adaptation is forced by repeatedly failing the same task: learning a new skill for the first time, or a new language from scratch, starts by first failing time after time. You need to learn how not to do it before you can understand how to progress and eventually become successful. How many times did you fall onto your soft-padded backside before you became sturdy enough to walk across the room, and then eventually hike mountains? How many times did you fall off your bicycle before you became competent enough to carry 50 newspapers in a bag on your back at 6 in the morning?

How many times did the nasty words hurt you from the school bullies before you psychologically developed the resolve needed to rise above it? Resilience is built from discomfort, not success.

To fail at something is a gift - a gift of knowledge. If you understand how to assess the failure and learn from it, then you can grow, adapt and evolve. The key word here is LEARN. Learn from the failure, don't fail at the lesson, "DON'T FAIL AT FAILURE".

Some believe we are at the peak of human evolution, when, in fact, studies show 10,000 years ago *homo sapiens*, meaning 'wise man' in Latin, were stronger, more intelligent, thicker boned, more agile and generally superior to modern day man in every way. Our overall gene pool is becoming weaker. We now live in a world where natural selection, survival of the fittest, strongest and most intelligent, has been taken away. Without meaning any disrespect, anybody can procreate in the new world; every human has equal rights. It's irrelevant whether your genes are an advantage or disadvantage to the evolution of *homo sapiens*. The genetic malfunctions within the creation of a new generation no longer come down to natural selection. Everyone has a chance; every misalignment has the opportunity to survive three further generations and become part of the human code. We are no longer evolving but devolving. Another way of saying it would be that we are still evolving, but negatively.

There are a few examples of when evolution happened in reverse. The most common one would be the penguin. The penguin evolved to be a bird of flight but has now lost this ability because it has given way to more muscle, more fat, denser bones and shorter, stiffer wings. This enables them to survive in the harsh climate of Antarctica and improves their manoeuvrability and sustainability in water. So, you could say that, in this case, the reverse in evolution was a benefit, given that their food source was underwater and not in the skies. Another reverse in evolution which scientists are confused about, is why birds lost their teeth, especially when most of them are carnivores. How is a beak more of an advantage than teeth when ripping apart a dead animal in the savannahs of Africa?

Neanderthals existed for around 300,000 years, and *homo erectus*, meaning 'standing man', who were our ancestors, lived for an incredible 1.3 million years. In both these forms, and many other human forms that existed before and alongside these, the evolution was awfully slow. In fact, there was truly little change during the length of their whole existence. They became part of the world around them, living in harmony with nature, giving back as much as they took, and were an integral part of the global circle of life. It does make you wonder, and worry greatly, when you look at what we have done with our mediocre 150,000 years of existence as *homo sapiens*. When you take into consideration how much we have evolved in such an unprecedented short amount of time, and the amount of damage we have caused along the way, what does the future hold? We no longer live within the circle of life - we've dominated and manipulated it for our own benefit. We are globally failing right now. What sort of planetary evolution will this force? As mentioned, most adaptations come when a force against it is too uncomfortable to deal with. We are making nature extremely uncomfortable. We are so transfixed on our growth and progression that we have neglected to see how many failures we are leaving in our wake. Nature continues to try and educate us about our wrongdoings, but we continue marching forward, trying to become gods ourselves, believing that our few measly years on the planet knows better than billions of years of evolution. How can we learn if we refuse to see and listen? Just like a balloon, we are expanding with such a force that my fear is we will very soon pop. This is the most important "DON'T FAIL AT FAILURE".

All failures and successes generate an endless complexity of hormones that initiate the necessary biological reaction to either maintain homeostasis or force an adaptation for survival. Homeostasis is the ability to maintain a relatively stable internal state that remains the same, despite changeable influences from the outside world.

There are 50 hormones floating around a human body in an ever-changing ratio, reacting to the influences of the environment around us, all performing remarkable tasks, and releasing when necessary from the eight glands spread throughout the body. This accumulation of glands and hormones is what we call our endocrine system. Hormones are messengers that instruct the activity of another part of the body. You probably know the name of some of these hormones: Insulin - the hormone released from the pancreas that regulates sugar in the blood by instructing muscle cells, liver cells and fat cells to open their doors and accept the excess sugar from the blood when too much sugar has been consumed because of our diet choices, maintaining homeostasis. Adrenaline - a hormone released into the blood when extreme stress is felt, providing goliath levels of strength or speed. It's the fight or flight hormone enabling the ability to escape harm or fight for your life. It's such a powerful hormone that, if you reached a state of extreme stress every single day, the volume of adrenaline collected during an 80 year lifespan would only fill a quarter of a thimble. What about the male and female hormones oestrogen and testosterone? These influence reproductive tissues, muscle growth and other tissues, and greatly affect mood, drive and aggression.

Often, people believe that variants in hormone releases will be dictated by mood. When you're happy, enthusiastic, calm or content, then the hormones which would be released into the blood would be the happy hormone cocktail of serotonin, endorphins, oxytocin and dopamine. Similarly, if you were angry, stressed, feeling either small or large levels of discomfort, then you would release the stress hormones cortisol and adrenaline. I believe it's six of one and half a dozen of the other. Your mood will produce a hormone release, which in turn reflects on your mood, sending you in either a downward or upward spiral of emotions. When you're down, you become negative about everything. Work becomes difficult, you see everyone's small irritations as big issues, the house is a mess, and even that knife in the spoon section of the cutlery drawer can ruin a weekend. If you're anything like me, then I guarantee you have experienced a very pissed-off mood but cannot explain why. There's no reason behind it, you're just aggravated. When you're flying high, smiling at everyone passing by, dancing whilst washing the dishes, then nothing can bring you down. This is when you're in the right place to feel the need to improve yourself. You spend time food prepping, you become interested in learning a new skill, you find the energy to strive for that promotion, and you appreciate the amazing spectrum of colours that autumn brings whilst venturing across a local field. Hormones can just as easily dictate our lives as much as we can influence which hormones are dominating.

The problem with hormones is that they still believe we are cave dwellers and react as they have for hundreds of thousands of years. They don't understand the modern world we now live in. If you are training hard in an air-conditioned gym on the perfectly engineered, extravagant equipment, hormones don't understand this. They think you are building a shelter or chopping wood, and they react to this stimulant by releasing the hormones for energy production, energy consumption, and muscle repair and growth. If you find yourself jogging or sprinting through the streets of your local town, hormonally you are hunting down your next meal or sprinting away from a tiger. They have evolved to protect us from influences and dangers that could harm or kill us. They have given us our sixth sense to know when something doesn't feel right, and we need to remove ourselves from our current environment. They make us feel love, attraction, hunger, thirst, despair, anxiety; every emotional state you can imagine. Every second of your life you are in a specific mindset because you feel you must be, for no reason other than it suits the occasion, not realising you can influence the hormonal reaction as much as it's influencing you. When you understand that the despair, anger or stress is just a hormonal release, then you learn that you just need a different hormone release. Playing bouncy music and dancing, taking a hot shower, or maybe just making a phone call to an upbeat friend, can change which, and how, the hormones influence your mood. Hormones do not understand the future, they don't understand the consequences of the past, and they can only react to the influences that live in the present, millisecond by millisecond. So, depending on how you deal with your current situation will inevitably develop into a rollercoaster of emotions that will affect your decisions of everything that happens after. An upward or downward spiral!

We have spoken about Melvin. Melvin's voice comes from a primitive part of the brain, nicknamed the monkey brain. It's Melvin that controls the hormones. It's Melvin that decides how you should react to a specific situation to limit the chance of death, harm or discomfort. During our evolution over the last 1.5 million years, our rational thinking brain has developed its own voice: a voice that understands consequence, a voice that remembers past events and predicts future possibilities.

This new brain then tells Melvin how to react to something that can't be changed from our past or something that might never happen in our future. This creates unnecessary stress and anxiety. If we can learn to distract our rational thinking brain with positive influences like music, dance, laughter, meditation, exercise, or just a good old chat with a friend, then we can change the conversation our rational thinking brain has with Melvin, reversing the downward spiral.

The duties required from cortisol and adrenaline have evolved because of physical and emotional failings our ancestors experienced. Generation after generation of family members and loved ones were hurt or killed thousands of years ago from sabre tooth tigers, venomous spiders and snakes, and poisonous berries, along with a multitude of other possible hazards and dangers, creating stress. This stress required an answer, something that would give you more of a fighting chance to survive. Cortisol was the answer. Cortisol being dumped into the blood became a friend; this powerful hormone awakened all the senses and raised the red flag when a threat or a danger could be imminent. The rustle in the leaves from one hundred yards away could now be heard. Hairs on your forearms now felt a change in wind direction. A deviation in grass movement across the meadow was now noticed by your peripheral vision, and you could now smell a predator upwind. Even your taste buds woke up with excitement in the anticipation of maybe fresh food coming from a kill. Adrenaline was then put on standby to sit on the side-lines, ready to pounce if the shit was really going to hit the fan. Our ancestors who reacted more efficiently to the stress hormones, using them constructively, lived longer. Failure to react productively to a stressful situation: for example, freezing like a rabbit in the headlights, could more often than not result in death. Stress hormones became a massive key to the survival, adaptation and evolution of our gene pool. Trust them and trust your instincts. If something doesn't feel right, it isn't. Your rational thinking mind is only as old as your calendar age. Your hormones are hundreds of thousands of years old, with amazing survival instincts.

As mentioned above, we now live in a totally different world where the dangers of being eaten by a tiger are all but eliminated. But our hormones don't know that. They are still reacting in the same way to emotional, physical or chemical stresses. Running out of coffee or even drinking the coffee, arguing with your teenage kids, realising the car is low on fuel when you are already late for work or missing a deadline for your boss, have the same release of stress hormones as being hunted through the long grass by a lion. The failure we are now facing in the 21st century is the ignorance of how damaging these hormones are now becoming. This low-level state of stress we all constantly live in, will maintain a level of alertness equivalent to spending 14, 16 or even 18 hours a day feeling we are being preyed on in the meadows where we once lived. It can be helpful to be on edge for minutes or even a couple of hours at a time when you're hunting, gathering or surviving, but to spend your entire conscious day fully alert, on edge, and ready to fight or fly is dangerously unhealthy. Increases in cancers, heart disease, diabetes and obesity, along with many, many other health conditions, both physical and mental, can be blamed, in part, on this constant drip, drip, drip of cortisol into your blood.

What's the answer? If your levels of stress hormones are high, and you find you constantly live a life full of pressure and unwanted burden, hormonally you're prepared to fight or run every day, all day, then the answer is obvious. Allow yourself to do just that. Work out, lift some stuff, run, swim, jump about, climb or dance. Anything to use those stress hormones for the job they were created for. Rolling around on a gym floor or fighting a tiger is exactly the same to your stress hormones; it releases the tension. Running, cycling or swimming will lower the stress hormones in the same way as chasing your prey to supply some much-needed nutrition for your family. Why do you think you feel calm, content and balanced after exercise? The tension being carried in your cardiovascular system has been used for exactly the purpose it was evolved for.

So, why failure?

There is far more to learn from failure. Growth happens more efficiently when you live as much of your life as possible just outside of what's comfortable, just at that point where failure and success pivots. Life is too comfortable and too fluffy now. We barely need to raise our heart rate or break a sweat to exist and survive, but is that enough for happiness? I want to send a message to my children and anyone else who's listening or reading. There is a huge difference between living and existing, and I'm fairly sure we weren't given this precious gift just to exist. I want them to understand that to live requires an element of failure, then to learn from it and to try again. The more you push yourself, the more you will fail. The more you fail, the more opportunity you will have to evolve. The more you evolve, the more reward you will feel from this amazing world and the life you've been given.

Chapter 8
My C.V.

Returning from Canada unsuccessful struck me deeply. The 2013 6633 Arctic Ultra was a massive lesson I just wasn't ready to learn or even accept; after all, I had smashed the Just Walk in May 2011. Then I conquered the National 3-peaks with nearly four hours to spare, changed my perception of what was possible whilst becoming one of the elite 5-dayers trekking 192 miles across the country. Lastly dragging myself around the 'Grim Reaper' for 100 miles in less than 26 hours, when even the organiser of the event whispered in my ear, "you shouldn't have finished this race", which I'll be covering in chapter 12. For weeks afterwards, all I could hear was a repeating stuck record nagging at my pride and knitting its way into my very being, teasing me as it whispered, "I don't fail!" "How did I fail?" "That wasn't supposed to happen".

Previously, reading books, watching documentaries and listening to podcasts was how I improved my knowledge, health and lifestyle, thus, enabling me to grow and improve in most aspects of my life. But, this new pain, and the feeling of overwhelming destruction that came from experiencing my first physical failure felt like I needed to start again from the very beginning. I lost confidence, self-respect, drive, and ambition. I didn't want to go to work, clean our house, or make any form of effort with any of my relationships. There was no point. I wasn't the person I perceived I was. I wasn't special, I had no skills, I didn't stand out as the madman people around me labelled me as. I needed proof that I was still worth something. I needed to find a way back. I needed to know I was still different.

One thought that stayed with me was, where was my little helper in Canada? Where was that hidden part of my character that felt invincible? When I was lying in the sleeping bag on the ice feeling destroyed, where was Melvin? Why didn't he show himself this time as he did on the Coast to Coast when my back was against the wall, and then again on the Grim Reaper, three months later. Why didn't he help me; how do I retrieve him? Was he gone forever? We needed to be re-acquainted, I needed to know he was still available if things went wrong. There was no other option; another race had to go on the calendar, but fear controlled the keys on the laptop, and I was unable to press the 'purchase' button that would enter me into a race.

It wasn't until the New Year when I eventually found the courage to book another challenge. Still very apprehensive, I registered for another Grim Reaper after successfully completing one hundred miles within the 26-hour time limit in the September following the Coast-to-Coast. Believing that if I were to find myself again and have a word with my alter ego, it would be best to go somewhere I last saw myself and Melvin. It was July 2014, and I was back at Grimethorpe Castle waiting for the gun to sound and releasing the anticipation of another 200 athletes. This time, I encouraged a large group of willing friends to join me from the Martial Arts studio where I was studying: every one of them hoping to achieve their first ultra-distance success. I had two goals, firstly to finish the 100 miles within 24 hours, and secondly, to rekindle the relationship with my old friend.

I understand now, six years later, that my alter ego has this amazing strength when the shit hits the fan. When a situation comes down to pure survival, pure instinct, he's your man. The problem is, the smart little monkey knows the difference between being in real trouble, and when you can be persuaded to falter and save all that unnecessary effort. And that's exactly what happened this time. I was injured in the Arctic which made it a very easy win for Melvin and now that he had a taste for winning, he had the upper hand. He knew how to keep me on the ropes; he knew the precise buttons to press to prevent me from giving it my all and he knew the difference between real trouble and when I was just looking for a bit of help. He knew the threat of injury was an easy way to get me to quit, so he took it, and used it to work against me.

Thirty-eight miles into my second year of 'The Grim Reaper', the darkness came down which triggered Melvin to start shouting. "I wasn't supposed to be here. This is stupid; why do you feel the need to prove to everyone you're a machine - nobody gives a shit", he whispered in my ear. It took a grand total of just five strides before I knew I was pulling out, but I couldn't just quit, I needed a reason. I couldn't just walk off. How could I face all my comrades who'd made a huge effort in training and preparations to join me if I just said, "I don't want to do this anymore". How could I save face? How could I make them believe it wasn't my fault? The answer came just as quickly as the problem did. I realised I needed an injury, and with that, I threw myself onto the gravelled path cutting my knees, thigh and hands, then staggered the last mile to the checkpoint and into the aid station. Once there, they cleaned me up and took some vital stats. Blood pressure was good 122/69, heart rate normal 73 bpm, awareness and reflexes were spot on. Then the big question came from the medical support, "are you ready to continue?" Shit, why did you have to ask that, I thought. "Yes", I reluctantly replied. My plan to be pulled out of the race had failed. "Great, let's take your stats once again and you can be on your way", they insisted. This time blood pressure read 96/52, and heart rate had dropped to 56.

This is actually my normal range, but I didn't let them know that and it raised concerns for the medics. They decided to pull me from the event due to such a dramatic drop. YES! I was out of the race and I didn't need to lose face. Everyone was sympathetic and supportive about my unnecessary and forced departure.

Once home after celebrating everyone else's successes at the Grim Reaper, I disappeared inwards again. I had no urge to train or push myself, and exercise became a disappointing chore. For weeks I had a short temper, useless as a husband and a father, and even walking the dogs turned into a daily argument. After ruining Christmas and then making it up to everyone, it took another New Year, crossing over into 2015, before I knew I had to pick myself back up. Staying defeated and broken wasn't going to work if I was going to continue being the best I could in all the other aspects of my life. I needed a new plan. I began thinking it was maybe because Melvin had known what was coming in The Grim Reaper, which made it easy for him to win once again. So, the plan was to find a new, different type of race. I looked at an A-B race; something that would scare and surprise him; something that would trigger a pure survival response, encouraging his help rather than his hindrance. After searching the web, I entered the 'South Downs Way 100' or 'SWD100'; a straight-line A-B event which took on 100 miles of the South Downs Path. Some of the route was the same as the 'Just Walk' event I finished with Gyula in 2011, and I knew the area was amazingly scenic, which could only help. This is one of the major 100-mile events in the UK. It's a qualifier for some of the harder, more extreme events around the world: The 'Western State Ultra' in California, The 'UTMB' in the Alps, and 'The Spartathlon' in Greece, among others. All of which I have dreamt of participating in if I ever had the opportunity to qualify for them. June came and I felt ready. I developed a training programme and kind of stuck to it; well, probably 60% of it, which was impressive for me. I was slowly learning, but I knew I could have done more. At least I'd built up to a few 40-mile walkie/jogs. I was feeling positive and enthusiastic. It was a beautiful summer's day, a nice temperature with a refreshing, cool breeze. Standing at the start I could already picture myself crossing the other end of the route victoriously. Teri was my support crew, meeting me at planned locations along the way. This helped immensely, making the breakdown of the event into small chunks a lot easier as I looked forward to our next hug. Fifteen hours into the race and 72 miles covered, I came up to the back of the van joyfully anticipating our next hug. I was comfortably ahead of schedule, reducing some of the pressure; so, I sat in the back for a few minutes, filled my belly and left in good spirits, and only feeling the muscle and joint pains you should expect at that stage. Melvin had made an appearance a few times, trying to convince me how dangerous this was and how I was going to create lasting injuries, but I'd managed to shut him up. Four miles further on, I jogged into an official checkpoint where I grabbed a quick, sweet cup of tea before rolling on. It was around 82 miles, just a mile or so shy of meeting Teri again that it went wrong. It was a dark night and head torches were very much necessary. When a light from behind cast my shadow out in front of me, I turned around to see who, or what, it was. Three racers joyfully came up behind me, chatting as if they were out for a casual Sunday morning cruise. Good old Melvin took this as an opportunity to stop me. I glanced up towards their head torches as they passed, leaving my vision impaired as if I'd glimpsed at the sun before returning to the darkness. This deterioration in vision grew until total blackness was left, and I found myself standing in the middle of a vast field with no idea of my surroundings and confused at which way to walk. I couldn't even see my feet or any silhouettes of trees and bushes in the moonlight. I checked my torch but couldn't make out if it was working or not. I guess the little monkey had become so desperate, after so many previous failed attempts to thwart my success. Last chance saloon for him was to take my sight. If I can't see, I can't progress. If I can't progress, I may as well quit and go home. A phone call to Teri explaining the situation resulted in me holding my ground whilst Teri walked out to meet me, then guided me back to the van. I was once again a DNF (did not finish). My sight didn't return until 12 hours later waking up in my bed the next day.

I was so close, over 80% through the race in a little under 17 and a half hours. What a kick in the balls, but at least I knew I had a sub-24-hour, 100 miles in me. So, without hesitation, I enrolled in the sister race of the SDW100, which is the NWD100 (North Downs Way 100). This was obviously further north than its southern sister and ran in a similar direction about 20 miles away, and as it was eight weeks later, I had plenty of time to repair and rebuild.

Again, standing amongst 300 others in anticipation of the starting pistol, and with Teri as my crew, I was set for another attempt at the 100 miles in 24 hours crown. This time, though, there were no dramatics, no real story to tell, no real excuses. I ran comfortably for 30 miles and decided I couldn't be bothered, so just walked off the race. I had no injuries, no issues, just the simple mindset that I didn't want to do it. I didn't want to be there; such an easy victory for my little friend. This was now four victories in a row for Melvin. He was becoming stronger with every race and quitting was becoming easier.

A couple of months later, however, I did finish a race - The Leicester Marathon; the first marathon I had ever entered. I had completed a few halves during training, but never an organised marathon. Finishing in four hours eleven minutes, I took the small victory and went home with a smile on my face. Whilst jogging around the north of Leicester's countryside, I came to the conclusion that the glory of the 100 miles was just beyond my genetics and decided to have a crack at a 100 km distance instead, thinking that could be my forte. Signing up for 'The Race to the Stones' lifted my spirits, it felt like a fresh start with a new focus. This is a 100 km, very scenic, A-B race. Very popular and included the perfect historic finish line of 'Stonehenge'.

The race takes place in the middle of July, and the weather told us as much. The mercury passed 30C (90F) for most of the day. Teri, a glutton for punishment, supported me once again. Truth be told, I just enjoyed this time we spent together as we didn't get much time on our own, and she is always supportive when it comes to my challenges. She always knows the right thing to say when I need a push and knows when a hug is the better choice to lift me back to my feet so I can keep me moving forward. All was going well for about 20 miles. It was around this distance that the heat started taking its toll. I couldn't drink enough; my guts had already given up. The more I drank, the more intense some newly-felt lower back pains started developing. At 30 miles I noticed that the pressure of my shorts pressing on my back became too much to bear. This wasn't Melvin, this was something else, and I started believing I did actually have a problem this time. Pulling out was absolutely the only right thing to do.

A week later the pain was still aggravating my back, and my normally slow urine stream had virtually come to a stop. Pee breaks now took five minutes as the urine just dripped. A visit to the doctors and then the hospital resulted in surgery where they burnt away some scar tissue that had made a home inside my urethra, blocking my urinal track. My kidneys had become very inflamed as my bladder backed up because I was unable to release all my urine. Apparently, even after I had squeezed out what

I could, one litre of urine remained in my bladder, and this angered my kidneys. If I had continued in this condition for another week or so, I would have been in very serious trouble.

The operation went well, and once I had managed to painfully allow 300 millilitres of urine out, I was homeward bound for a couple of weeks rest. That was the plan anyway, but as we all know, plans don't always go as planned. Less than twenty-four hours later we were heading back to the same hospital, but it wasn't for me this time, it was Teri. As I was incapacitated, enjoying being nursed on the sofa and catching up on some box sets, Teri was painfully busy, doing what she could around the house. As she was rushing through the house, she pushed the spare room door open with her foot whilst carrying a basket of clean clothes, not realising the door was secured in its frame, and broke her foot. My two weeks of required rest quickly came to an abrupt end as I drove her to the hospital. We were back home a few hours later with Teri in a hard plastic boot and a lot of pain, with specific instructions to rest for a few weeks.

I slowly did what I could with the day to day running of the house, being as careful as possible, but as you can imagine, things went further south. That evening, as I tentatively released the contents of my bladder, I felt a tear in my penis, the urine stopped flowing and I hit the floor screaming. The area of the urethra that had been lasered had ripped open and the urine was leaking into the flesh of my penis, making it swell. I'd never felt pain like it. A few seconds or maybe a lifetime later, depending on which side of the experience you were witnessing, the pressure released and left me lying on the floor in a two-foot-wide puddle of blood-infused urine. Four hours later I'd returned from the hospital after being told they couldn't do anything without worsening the situation and convincing me it would heal in time. I would spend hours crying over the next eight days as I stood in front of the toilet, reluctantly trying to answer the call of nature again and again. Every time I went through the same routine, which would leave me on the floor, grasping my groin in agony in a pool of blood and urine. I developed a very precise system of letting a little out, letting it go through the usual painful process, and then allowing a little more out, continuing the cycle until the bladder was empty. Then, strangely, on the ninth day, it just stopped. No more pain, no more blood, no more swelling; I could pee like a racehorse for the first time in 20 years. It was amazing. I continued to laugh every time I peed for days afterwards. I felt like Tom Hanks from the film, 'The Green Mile'. It's always the little things that create the most joy. A couple of weeks later, Teri's foot had also healed, and it was back to life as normal in the Humber household.

After enjoying a nice family Christmas with the girls, and both of us fully recovered, it was time to book something once again. Booking the year's antics as another year started had developed into a habit; maybe it was my way of getting over the January blues. A couple of half marathons in the spring to wake up the legs for the summer, and the Leicester Marathon again in October as it was an easy marathon, as far as marathons go, and just down the road, but I still needed the main event. The completion of the first Grim Reaper was starting to feel like a bit of a fluke. The 100 miles was eating at me and I was losing confidence with each race.

I found an event called 'Equinox24'; similar to the Grim Reaper as it was in loops, but 10 km loops instead of 10 miles, and it was a limitless endurance race. The idea, simply, is to run as many laps as possible in 24 hours. This is it, I thought. I know I can do laps - no pressure - I can take my time. Sixteen laps and I've nailed the 100 miles. It's only half hour drive away and includes free camping for all the family for the whole weekend. Perfect. A weekend away for the support crew...I mean family, thrown in!

The atmosphere was amazing. It was totally different from any event I have been to; almost like a festival. We pitched our big, six berth tent next to the track for easy access between laps, and the four of us went for a stroll around the camping field to check in for the race, and to look through some of the stalls stocking running gear. Music bellowed from all directions; people were buzzing around the campsite trying to find friends, and money was exchanging hands as Sunday fun runners spent hundreds on new performance-enhancing clothing and equipment. There was an amazing variety of food venues set up in a huge circle, with tables in the middle. Chinese, burgers, big breakfasts, pizzas, hog roast, coffee and snacks; even a beer bus. The main event was to start the next day, Saturday, at 12.00 noon. Friday evening brought everyone together for some fun and food, and one of the fun races was a beer run. Participants would stand on the start line with a pint of their favourite beverage, and on the sound of the pistol, they would drink their pint as quickly as possible, followed by a one-mile lap around the outside of the camping area. This was also the last mile of the 10 km route. It wasn't long before we started seeing the beverages again; the Guinness, especially, didn't look pleasant coming back up. Our tent was perfectly placed at the point where stomachs started rebelling, so we had a great view of racers bent over with Niagara Falls coming out of their mouths. All I could think of was that I had to run through that tomorrow.

Morning soon came, and after a kids' fun run, and the usual health and safety talk, noon was upon us and we were off. Being set in the grounds of Belvoir Castle, the course itself didn't disappoint, with mixed terrain between grass, gravel and tarmac; quite undulating and with the pleasure of running past all the camping support on the last mile. The support was great, but the countless BBQs made breathing a little difficult as you inhaled a lungful of smoke. The target was 16 laps, and after seven, I was feeling good. Myia decided to join me for a very enjoyable eighth, mostly walking with an occasional jog. Then Teri supported me on the ninth and tenth. I loved that my wife was now able to do this, remembering the days in the wheelchair. Unfortunately, I loved it so much I stopped after the tenth lap, convincing myself I couldn't go back out on my own and would prefer to enjoy a meal out under the stars with Teri at midnight. Still, 100 km in 12 and a half hours isn't anything to be disappointed with. It was an enjoyable weekend; I spent time with my family and came away with no injuries. One of my most favourite events so far, and re-confirming 100 km as my distance. Not my nemesis, the 100 miles.

I then went on to finish the season with a personal best in Leicester, my first sub-four-hour marathon. I passed the finish line at Victoria Park with three hours and fifty-six minutes on the clock. Running allows a lot of time for thinking; it's why I call it my meditation time. Whilst walking the last mile of the marathon, I questioned whether I should just concentrate on marathons. They don't take up so much time, they are still very credible and even if I cock one up, I know I can still walk it out.

The next two years were littered with Marathons: another Leicester Marathon, as well as Milton Keynes, Athens, London and Berlin, along with plenty of halves and one last attempt at the 100 miles. I returned to the Equinox the year after, but once again I convinced myself I couldn't progress past the 10th lap. I did however achieve a new PB on the 100 km – a proud 11 hours 30 minutes.

The weather during the Milton Keynes marathon was horrifically hot, maybe touching 34C (100F). It was halfway through the race when my systems started shutting down. Peeing was painful, I developed diarrhoea, and eventually was sick on the twenty-third mile marker; but I continued, finishing in a brilliant stadium as people cheering from their seats as the clock ticked over three hours fifty-three minutes. Not a bad event, and very enjoyable if it wasn't for the heat of that day, and with a fantastic finish line in the MK Football Stadium.

November 2018 included the day I stood at the start line of the authentic Athens Marathon with my Sunday morning running buddy, Karen. We spent hours most Sundays putting the world to rights and talking about future events we would both like to do. One Sunday morning, she stirred up some jealousy when she announced she was off to Athens to take part in the original marathon; the place where the marathon started. It was Pheidippides who, in 490 BC, ran roughly twenty-five miles from Marathon to the centre of Athens to announce the defeat of the Persians. So, with this jealousy and excitement, I bounced back home with our usual celebratory coffee in hand, and without hesitation booked a lovely weekend away with Teri to Athens: which, of course, included a marathon in the middle. I loved Athens; we both did. I loved the culture, and I loved the history, but the marathon itself wasn't my favourite. For 99% of the race, it was a straight dual carriageway from A-B, steadily increasing in ascent for the first 20 miles. The last remaining one percent of the race was unquestionably worth the effort though: probably my favourite one percent of all my races. The finish line was in the 2700-year-old Olympic Panathenaic Stadium, where the Olympic games originated, and where all the athletes would have to compete naked. This nakedness was necessary, firstly to appreciate and celebrate the male physique as Spartans would spend hours everyday training in calisthenic exercises to achieve a beautiful body, (this is what the word calisthenics means, 'beautiful body'), and secondly, as a tribute to the gods. I didn't feel the need to celebrate my body or send a tribute to any god that day, so I stayed comfortably covered in my Adidas drapes. It was a tough race, especially with the heat; even though it was November the temperature started creeping up from 9am, reaching 27C by mid-afternoon. Shuffling over the line in three hours forty-four minutes, feeling physically damaged as normal, but this time it was deeper than just the muscles. The difference was how mentally damaged I felt. I was in a bad way, dipping in and out of consciousness on the side of the road for over an hour before managing to find Teri. Concerned, she supported me back to our apartment where I slept for a few hours, waking up quite confused. I didn't think too much of it at the time, and just continued to shovel down a few thousand calories before enjoying a night out with Karen, her husband, Alan, and a few new faces.

London was next; my first experience of a major marathon. There are currently six majors, London, Berlin, Tokyo, New York, Chicago and Boston, and I was starting to tease myself with the idea of completing all of them, which would be an accolade in itself. But first things first; let's see how London felt. The day of the race was special; it was also my 46th birthday, which made for a nice gathering the night before with friends, including Karen and Alan again, but I still stuck with my own tradition of early to bed and early to rise as a pre-race routine. The morning came and the bustle around London was fantastic; I loved the energy in the city. In every direction, down every street and on every tube, there were athletes of all shapes and sizes, some donned in expensive lycra from all the famous running brands, and some dressed in an array of spectacularly colourful and imaginative costumes. I remember thinking, as I sat opposite someone on the tube, if that banana beats me, I really need to quit this game! As we entered Greenwich Park where most of the runners begin, I felt overwhelmed at the enormity of the event, thousands upon thousands of nervous, jittery, dazed individuals who were about to find out if they had done enough training, and about to experience the pain, discomfort and utter joy of accomplishing something they never thought possible. The gun started the 2019 London Marathon, and the crowd went nuts, and continued to go nuts for the whole day. It took twenty or so minutes before I crossed the start line, but once over the line, space appeared, and I could stretch my legs. This couldn't have come soon enough, because of my anxiety at being in a crowded situation. It had been bubbling away for an hour; I didn't like being so close to so many people. When this anxiety released as I crossed the start line, it went like a coiled spring. I was moving fast - too fast - I knew it but couldn't change it. I needed more space and ran into every opening available in front of me. The first 22 miles were a blur. I can't remember any of the mile markers or historic buildings. Considering my best-ever marathon was three hours thirty-nine minutes in Leicester, I became aware I was currently on target for a three-hour fifteen-minute finish, as I passed my first acknowledged mile-marker, the 22nd. This is where I woke up and snapped out of my dream-like state, thinking, I could actually get a 'good for age'. A good for age is a time you need to open up the doors for the opportunity to race other more prestigious races; one of those races being the Boston Marathon, another of the Majors. My 'good for age' at 46 years old was three hours twenty minutes. I was five minutes ahead and starting to feel victorious. Then, as it usually does, something went wrong.

Something broke. I can't put my finger on what, but it was sudden. I felt like I did at the end of the Athens marathon. I couldn't breathe properly; my heart felt angry, my legs turned to jelly, and my vision was blurred. From London Bridge to the end of the race at St James's

Park, approximately 4 miles, was very strange. I wasn't exhausted or fatigued like in other races, but I definitely wasn't present. The only way I can describe it was that I was broken. I couldn't even tell you if I was moving in the right direction. Crossing the finish line, claiming my medal over my head and being handed a goody bag, I was totally spaced out. All I could think of was getting to the letter M. This is where Teri and other help would be. The alphabet was spread out around the outside of the park to help meet friends and family after the race, and we chose the letter 'M' as a place to meet because I was raising money for a local charity called Menphys. They provide services and help for disabled children in the area. Confused and disoriented, I made it to 'M' 30 minutes after finishing to find absolutely nobody to support me. Where was the charity and where was Teri? I needed her more than ever. I had nothing left and started panicking. Next thing I remember I was sitting on the floor, leaning against the 20-foot-tall construction of the letter 'M' with a variety of unknown jackets and coats sprawled over me. I have no idea how long I had been there or how long it had taken before Teri found me, but when she did, all I can remember is bursting into tears and telling her I was broken. I could barely stand, never mind walk, but Teri managed to get me back onto my feet, returned the coats to a concerned family standing next to us, and dragged me out of the park. After a few cups of tea and a bite to eat, I slowly became compos mentis over the next few hours, but something was still wrong. I did manage another personal best of three hours thirty minutes, but there was no joy at the end.

Five months later I was squashed into another seat on another airplane on my way to another marathon, with Teri parked next to me. We were heading for the Berlin Marathon, something I had booked when I was thinking of doing all the majors before I went to London, but now had no interest in, whatsoever. I couldn't run anymore. I tried numerous times to get my legs back but continually felt damaged whenever my heart rate increased. Every attempt to run would make my chest tighten and my heart scream like a pulled muscle. Landing at Berlin Schönefeld Airport, my anxiety about the situation increased, driving me into a hole that I couldn't dig myself out from. I told Teri as soon as we found our accommodation that I wanted to go home. I didn't want to be here, and I wasn't going to do the marathon, but to save the weekend she persuaded me to stay, so we could at least experience the City and all its history.

Berlin has such a vast culture switch between the West and East, both with a very unique feel and atmosphere, both very intimidating, and both made me feel unwelcome, but I've ticked the city off my list and don't feel the need to return. I don't necessarily think it was the place, more to do with my anxiety about being there. The morning of the marathon arrived, and our intentions were to venture downtown and watch the event, but something made me get dressed for the occasion. Somehow, an hour later I was suited and booted for running a marathon, including my number on my shirt; still with the intention to merely watch. Entering the Tiergarten Park, the starting point of the race, Teri and I had to separate because she wasn't permitted past the barriers without a race number. I whispered in my wife's ear, "I'll be back shortly", further explaining I just wanted to have a look inside and feel the buzz. Before I knew it, the race had started, and I was involved. I started running; I don't know why, I just did. I even had to call Teri two miles into the race to tell her I had left the park and was running the marathon: "I'll see you in a few hours". For the 26.2 miles, I was baffled as to how I was even continuing. I just did one mile at a time, repeatedly telling myself, just do one more mile and then find your way back home to Teri. I finished in just over four hours, my second slowest time, but I finished without incident, apart from the damage I still felt in my chest from London. Another medal on the wall, another t-shirt for the drawer, and another Major ticked off.

The pain and anxiety in my chest continued for months. Time after time I would venture out for a few miles, returning 20 minutes later beaten. I didn't see the point in running anymore. I hated it, and very quickly accepted this part of my life was finished. I had a good run, pardon the pun, spending most of October, November and December in the gym, lifting weights and very little time on my feet running. This felt good on the body; my muscle mass increased by a few kilos, and there was a nice body shape developing, but mentally, I was falling. I didn't realise how much I relied on the fresh air and the hormonal reply from running. I also felt that finishing this chapter of my life in such a negative way, wasn't right. I couldn't leave it like this; I had to finish on my terms. This has been part of my life for 10 years and I have to finish on a high. Thus, a weekend-long conversation with Teri resulted in my Health Club sponsoring me to revisit the arctic once again to finish my biggest nemesis, the 6633 Arctic Ultra. With a 14-month training program pencilled in, it was time to get back on the horse. Let's finish this in style.

Chapter 9
Why?

Understanding some of the lessons I had learnt over the previous few years, I didn't want to finish this part of my life feeling like I hadn't given it my all. If full commitment wasn't given, then failing or succeeding was irrelevant; the end result didn't matter. I didn't want this to be the message I leave behind. I needed to show that success or failure is irrelevant if everything was given. This is what I want my children and future generations to understand. I needed to go back and do it again. I needed to show myself, more than anyone, that I was progressing and learning, and what a difference giving it your all makes. I needed to return to my biggest nemesis, the 6633 Arctic Ultra.

The decision to revisit the 6633 wasn't an easy one when you consider the amount of dedication to training and preparation needed to be successful, and the financial drain on our family's limited resources. But it was something very necessary before I was able to move on and step into a new chapter in my life. Currently, I had come to realise I still suffered from a level of depression which included bouts of anxiety. Reading a multitude of books and spending hours and hours self-analysing, I came to some conclusions. Firstly, I had lost my own identity. I didn't know who Stuart Humber was. I didn't have hobbies, I didn't know what I liked, I didn't know what I didn't like. I still woke up every day going from A to B to C, all the way to Z, doing exactly what needed to be done with military precision, and that was the problem. I just did things I had to do, instead of some things I wanted to do. Secondly, I discovered a few reasons why my parade of medals on the wall all were earned with a great deal of pain, and whether successful or not, they were all failures. Lastly, to know where my depression and various levels of anxiety issues came from, and how working on this could hopefully improve the impact they were having on my life.

Understanding these revelations, I looked a bit deeper into *WHY?*

At 27 years old I was like any other 27-year-old, believing I was the centre of the universe. Going from day to day centred around what I needed from my life. I knew I was a little more understanding than most when it came to other people's issues but had never been put in a situation where continued patience and empathy was needed.

When my relationship with Teri was in its infancy, we had deep discussions about her disabilities and the emotional rollercoaster she suffered because of it. I acknowledged and sympathised with her issues, agreeing to work hard around the house to make things easier and give her everything she needed to manage what she could in life. I broke down the daily routines into bite-size chunks to allow me to work through it in the same way a runner works through a marathon. You see, I have a very mechanical and mathematical brain. Problems always have an answer. I see things in black and white, making me very good at problem-solving, but not so good, I realised later, at empathy. Living with someone who has disabilities, I noticed more than ever that not everything is as clear as black and white; not everything necessarily needs fixing. Sometimes they just want you to understand, accept the situation for what it is, give them a shoulder and then move on. This intuition took years of unhappiness and arguments on both sides before empathy was added to my tool kit. I still believe I am a very good problem solver, but now I have this new ability to be empathetic to other people's problems. I believe this is one of the reasons I have a successful Health Club: I listen, assess, advise and encourage.

Unfortunately, the flip side of this newly-mastered empathy was that everyone wanted a piece, leaving no space to care for me. I had become so efficient at listening to people, showing empathy and then helping them by breaking things down into easy-to-manage chunks, that my needs slowly got pushed further and further down the list. I forgot I even had any, which I am sure you must have felt at some point in your life. As I said, it took years and years of aggressive arguments, falling out and being kicked out of the house to force a character change, making it possible for both of us to be happy in our life together.

Seventeen years later I realised I hadn't touched base with myself for such a long time that I didn't even know how to do it anymore. I was only comfortable caring, listening and fixing other people's problems. This dedication to caring, guiding, and supporting my house and my family made me very controlling. I had to be. I turned it into a 60 to 70 hour a week job. I became so efficient in my world, knowing every single second of every single day had a purpose and an objective, I couldn't accept anyone else making a decision or taking responsibility for a task that I needed to do myself. Eighteen hours of my day, every day, was regimentally performed so that everyone received what they needed and was as happy as I could make them.

The problem was that Teri, now able-bodied, had new hobbies. She climbed and hiked; she became a volunteer first responder in our town, supporting the NHS; she was back on horses and she was working again. My two daughters had grown up, now spending more time in their own space trying to understand who they were and how they would fit into this world, and repeatedly reminding me that they didn't require my constant attention and care anymore.

The role I had become so accustomed to had gone. The massive change in character I had gone through to become empathetic and put others first, was now redundant. It was very disturbing to sit on the sofa in the middle of a Saturday afternoon with no purpose, and equally as painful to hand some of life's responsibilities back to Teri.

Depression, anxiety, and resentfulness all crept back in; I didn't know what to do. I didn't know where I was supposed to be or who I was supposed to be. I still had clients at the club who looked to me for help and advice; they still needed lifting back to their feet, but it didn't give me the same fulfilment as looking after my small world. My strength to be empathetic, and to be a shoulder for clients to cry on, came from doing the same for my family. Losing this necessity to be strong for Teri and the girls made me less effective in my working life. I felt I could do better, and needed to do better, for them. This added to the void I was feeling.

Panic attacks were now catching me off guard daily. I could be at work, out shopping, watching a film in the cinema or running. I could be anywhere and would feel an overwhelming need to be in my house and in my bedroom. This is where I felt safe enough to regain control so I could carry on. Numerous times I would walk out of the supermarket or the cinema, quickly race home to safety and leave my family behind, only to return to pick them up once I had settled.

Crying on a Saturday afternoon became so normal that, whoever was nearest to me when I happened to need a release, held me until I stopped. This could happen whilst making dinner or washing the car, reading a book, or even just playing a game. Then, once calm, they would return to whatever they were doing without saying a single word. I explained to my girls that it was just the release I needed every week to be effective at helping others. Deep inside I knew that wasn't the case; there was something else.

I lived like this for a couple of years until realising that, if I didn't challenge this, I could lose everything. One morning I decided to walk around the local fields and try to talk to myself and break down what was going on. After all, this was my job.

This is how I made a living, helping others with the same issues. I was the bloody health guru; I'm not supposed to be like this. If I can't even fix myself, then everything I say to my clients must be bullshit and I must be a fake.

Without stating the obvious, my initial conclusion was that I needed to rediscover who I was; what did I like and what made me laugh. I needed to enjoy 'me' again. So, on returning, I sat Teri down and we had a very productive talk. I explained that the first 17 years of our relationship had changed me into something that was no longer needed. Her disability was a huge force that created this necessary change. Maybe I need something just as influential to force an adaptation the other way, something I can get my teeth into and do just for me; something that will allow me to rediscover myself and spend a lot of time becoming reacquainted with myself. This is why I chose to head back to the 6633, but do it properly this time, applying everything I had learnt from failures and successes in my life - everything I have learnt through reading 200 plus books on health, diet, fitness, motivation and development.

If I could gather everything I had been through, all the growth, change, strength and resilience I had mastered from looking after a disabled wife, raising a couple of amazing kids, maintaining a home, holding down a 60-hour-a-week job and performing in numerous races successfully or not; collect it all into a ball and use it as an energy to drive me through a year of dedicated training, what could I achieve? What could I find out about myself? Would I find a new direction?

I would definitely have all the time I needed to figure these questions out whilst covering thousands of miles during training, then over another 383 miles of solitude on the actual event. It seemed the perfect answer to rekindle my self-awareness.

I started training immediately. Miles started increasing and as expected, I spent a lot of time talking to myself and talking to Melvin. I enjoyed listening to my music again. I changed my usual audio educational books to motivational stories about climbing Everest or ultra-running. I read or listened to any book where someone had put themselves up against the odds of an extreme challenge which required unquestionable resilience. I was starting to feel joy in myself and spending time with myself. I performed better at work; I was happier around the house. The weekend ritualistic crying stopped, and panic attacks relented. Things were happening as I had hoped they would.

Then it happened, the Covid 19 lockdown. Within days I hit the floor again, thinking I was going to lose the business. After five years of blood, sweat and tears, I had only just built it up enough to provide a slightly more comfortable life. Twenty percent of members pulled out instantly. I couldn't guide my private clients, and for the first time in my adult life, I wasn't working. I didn't realise how long an actual day was when you have nothing to put in it. I would get up, walk for a couple of hours, clean the house, then the garage and the car, eat some food and go to the supermarket. Then, after all that, I looked at my watch and it wasn't even midday. What do I do now? What should I do tomorrow? After two weeks I found myself waking up one morning at 3am staring at the ceiling, convincing myself I was going down, and I didn't want to take my family with me. So, with that, I sat up, got dressed, jumped into the car and started to drive with the intention of never coming back. I managed to drive a few junctions up the motorway before coming to my senses and returning home. Another deep conversation with Teri was needed, but I didn't really know what to say, so went for my daily two-hour walk to once again analyse my actions.

It's amazing how much of a fantastic ear Mother Nature has. If you ever have a problem, just go and talk to her for a bit, on your own.

Being unable to go into work opened my eyes to how reliant I was on it; how much of a hold it had on me. I had always said from an early age that I would only work to have a life, not to make work my life. I had been dedicating 60 to 70 hours every week to my work for 15 to 20 years, not realising how much of an impact that was having until it was taken away. With this new awareness, I understood I needed to pass some of the weight onto Sylvia, and I also employed another part-time helper, Charlee.

I had seen Charlee around the town and followed her on social media. I knew she had a fantastic work ethic and showed a natural dedication to helping people. She is young, excited, loves training, and comes from a different exercising background, which complimented my style and provided variation to our community. Adding to our unit allowed me to reduce my hours to a more manageable 45 to 50 hours per week, thus giving me some selfish time to work on myself.

Who knows, maybe Covid has prevented me from having a heart attack in 10 years?

Over the coming months, adding mile after mile, doing press up after press up and pull up after pull up, I questioned so many things about myself. Why I continued with the same habits; why I behaved in specific ways; how I made others feel around me, and why I made myself feel the way I did.

One question that regularly popped up was, why did I continue to approach races in the same way, time after time, knowing it would result in the same outcome – failure? It was mainly, my quest to complete 100 miles in 24 hours. What made it possible for me to battle through my first attempt at the 100 miles and finish it, when I was totally underprepared, and why couldn't I replicate it?

The only explanations I have for some of these questions would have to come from looking closely at my life at that time, and my relationship with it. Building up to the first Grim Reaper my journey was hard, depressing and dark. I struggled minute by minute, day by day and year by year with the emotional challenges I would have to endure just to get to the next obstacle. This heavy, dark cloud needed a release. I desperately needed to discharge, to let go of everything I was holding in. All that pain, all that discomfort, and all that anger. The further I progressed through the 100 miles, the more tension was released, in the exact same way a self-harmer would cut themselves with a knife to feel a reprieve from their current situation. The determination to finish the race for the charity, to be victorious when the odds were stacked against me, and the need to earn the respect and inspirational accolades everyone told me I gave them when they heard about my success, was actually a discreet way of self-harming. It was a very clever, hidden and selfish form of physical self-sabotage. The more pain I felt, the more the internal voices were silenced. There was no more emotional baggage cluttering my vision. As I forced myself on through blisters, agonising joints and painfully swollen feet, taking step after step, the physical pain became so much more powerful than the physiological pain. It became an ally and a friend who would give sanctuary from the 18 to 20-hour days of responsibility and control I carried with me every day of my life. The pressures of my daily duties felt like a continuous, slow drip of water softly hitting the exact same spot on my forehead; and this, during race day, would be distracted by the agony in my hips, my feet and my back. That relentless drip that started out being quite manageable for the first hour or two, would grow, and continue to grow day after day, turning into a torturous act, sending me into some very dark places. The relief came when self-inflicted damage was done by racing; racing until I felt like someone had hit my feet with a hammer, and blood was coming from random places. This gave me a much-needed respite from the drip, drip, drip, drip, of my life.

Another question then arose from this realisation; could this be the reason why I didn't train as much as I should for my events? If I were sufficiently prepared for a race, would it hinder my therapeutic reason for participating in the race in the first place? I believe the answer is yes. Being better prepared would mean less psychological damage. Could this also be the reason, or at least contribute to the reason, why I had so many DNFs after the first Grim Reaper? I would enter every race with a goal. This goal, I assumed, would have been just like everyone else's on the start line, which was to compete or complete the challenge. But maybe mine was a little different; maybe I needed something deeper. Maybe mine was to reach a specific level of discomfort. This level of pain could either be felt during the race or from the dissatisfaction of failing the race. Maybe failing was the sadistic pain I needed to not feel the drip, drip, drip, of the tap; even just for a short time.

This is pretty deep stuff, and I make no apologies, but this is the exact reason I had to return to the 6633 ultra. For the first time, I had entered a challenge for the excitement, pleasure, growth and accomplishment I would feel at the end. I wasn't looking for a distraction from my pain, discomfort or sorrow. I wanted to return home after the event without injury, without any feeling of remorse, and without the satisfaction that the demons were temporarily silenced. There aren't any demons. I am returning to Canada for a few reasons, but one big one is to have an amazing adventure with a cracking story to tell.

I have discovered in recent years a love of telling a story and passing on information and knowledge. I can honestly say that passing on knowledge is the whole reason I have my club. It's not the exercise I direct people through on an hourly and daily basis; it's the stories I tell them whilst they are glowing, sweating and panting through the routine I've given them until they are exhausted. It's something I will never stop doing. In 50 years' time, I still hope I am capable of constructing wonderful, easy-to-understand stories that will wake up younger minds, helping them to progress in life healthier, with more contentment, full of passion, and the ability to give and receive love.

By revisiting and overcoming some old haunts like the 6633, the NDW100, the SDW100 and the Race to the Stones, I will give myself a brilliant story to tell. A story I can pass on to anyone willing to listen; a story full of growth, adaptation, self-awareness, coming of age, resilience, determination and passion. You see - PASSION - this is where the magic happens. This is what changes you from a caterpillar to a butterfly, and this is the difference between having an existence 'OR' living a life. PASSION is the key that makes you use words like laughter, enjoyment, excitement, devotion, gratitude, joy and love. Money, commercialism and materialism cannot complete you; only passion can: passion in your relationships, passion in your vocation, passion for nature, passion for the human spirit, and passion for self-fulfilment. This is life.

Everyone has passion. Some people's passion has been drowned by the unachievable expectations placed onto their shoulders by the system. Some people's passion is scared to raise its head above the smothering cloud of normality because of what others might say, but the lucky few live with their passion on their sleeve for all to see, and they live an exciting, spontaneous, plentiful and joyful life. This is because every day has purpose for them, and every achievement further fuels the passion inside. Unfortunately, these lucky ones, are few and far between, but they stand out like a sore thumb.

As you can see, I am deeply passionate about passion, which is why I now spend my time pursuing my dreams and leading by example in the hope that my daughters will be educated by it and driven to follow theirs. I believe that, when it comes to becoming a successful human and being successful in life, knowing yourself and being confident in who you are, what you like, what you dislike and what you are passionate about, is, above all else, crucial. You can work as hard as you can to build a respectable C.V. full of qualifications, work experience, and interesting hobbies, but if you don't have passion for what you have and what you're doing, it will niggle at your subconscious, eventually eating you up from the inside out. All those childhood dreams you once had that were full of excitement, knowing you had the world at your feet and a lifetime to experience it, have dwindled away into a ghostly shadow: a shadow that floats around its entire life partaking in an unfulfilling career, earning as much money as possible to buy as much stuff as it can, to try and fill the emptiness that's left behind when passion has left the building. This is not what I want for my cherubs, my two angels, and, as always, I educate by example. I want to show them how powerful passion can be; how much it can shape life and attract people. Regardless of where your passion takes you, if you show it, people will follow. Why? Because it's now in very short supply, and others will be attracted to you and long to be part of your life because you have it. By revisiting my past through these events, I am hopefully showing my daughters that even when things get tough and life is pulling you in 10 different directions, don't falter and don't sell out; see it through and follow your heart. That's how you live, and not just exist.

One of my passions is passing on knowledge. I love making people feel better. There is nothing that compares to the feeling you receive when someone has come into your day with low energy, no enthusiasm and heavy-shouldered, but then leaves revitalised, full of childhood excitement and a want for more out of life. This is my drug; this is what gets me out of bed in the morning. Just like any other drug, the need for bigger 'hits' inevitably comes. This is where I hoped this book, and my openness in this book, will help others. As much as I love my club and the people involved in it, I need more. I want to help more; I want to continue helping as many as possible and tell stories to as many people as possible.

Quite a few WHYs answered there; none of them more or less relevant than the other, but all thoroughly thought through. Now, with the *why* sorted, it was onto the *how*. Time to get sweaty!

Part 3
Time to Practice
What I Preach

Chapter 10
Training (Part 1)

January

Training started the moment I decided to commit to the race at the beginning of January 2020. The first focus was to start using my legs again. The London Marathon and the Berlin Marathon were the last two occasions I had covered anything over five miles, with London hurting me in a way that wasn't only physical, but psychological. I knew my body was now ok and fully capable of stepping it up, but there was now a new demon in the dark that needed exorcising. I knew that by challenging this demon, I could eventually feel comfortable leaving the house again. I still hated running; I didn't even want to walk. I'd only been averaging around 50 miles a month for months, and that was forced. Step by step I ventured further and further, using a weapon I have now come to love. Audiobooks: I can't get enough of them. Listening to Ant Middleton, David Goggins, Wim Hof, Bear Grylls, Ranulph Fiennes, and Ben Fogle amongst others, not only helped me through the 124 miles I accrued in January, but also, intermittently, throughout the whole year. They stopped me from feeling lonely and helped me overcome the slight agoraphobia I sometimes suffered. I still look back at January as being one of the toughest months to get through. But at least the ball was rolling. To keep the momentum moving forward in February, I decided to try increasing January's total by 25 miles. I did complete 142 and a half miles, just shy of the target that was 150. This provoked a process of adding a further 25 miles per month, every month, until distance training finished at the end of January the next year. It could be walked, jogged or run, and would require me to achieve a maximum of 425 miles in the January before cooling down in February in preparation for my departure to Canada. My fitness was still on point from plenty of circuits, but my body weight had increased by three and a half kilograms since London, as I had replaced most of my running hours with strength training.

February

At the beginning of February, through a visitor to the Club, I was directed to a social media friend of theirs called Jonny Davies. Jonny had finished the 6633 in 2015 and lived locally. After a short investigatory text, followed by a very quick response, we were having a coffee in his cafe, Cafe Ventoux, which is comfortably placed in a small but popular cycling village just outside Leicester. Jonny clarified that he had finished the 6633 in 2015 in a time of 182 hours and 30 minutes. He also offered his services to the directors of the race to become a medical officer on the race in 2016, 2017, 2018 and 2019, as he was a paramedic. I instantly realised how lucky this situation was. Not only did I have someone local who had completed the race, a very rare find indeed, but someone who had witnessed first-hand from the side lines why people fail or succeed. The big, and I mean huge breath-taker, was that Jonny had also recently enrolled in the 2021 race. He wasn't going to be the medical support, but a competitor; he was racing again. Why would someone go back to such a harsh and expensive race when they had already been successful once before?

Firstly, the route was now different. It had evolved into a different race. The original race was 352 miles; this was the route I attempted in 2013. That route is now unobtainable because the last 100 miles was along an ice road on the Arctic Ocean from Inuvik to Tuktoyaktuk, which melted away in the summer months and was remade each winter. During 2016 and 2017 a new land road was constructed linking the two towns, therefore removing the need for an ice road. So, from 2018 onwards a new route was planned which would include a third of the race on the Mackenzie River snaking up to Inuvik, then a hop, skip and a jump along the new 97-mile land road to Tuktoyaktuk. This new route totalled 383 miles, and Jonny wanted to add this distance to his CV.

The second reason was that he felt the new distance record was achievable and fancied a shot. Just for reference, the record of the original route was, and will always be, 5 days, 23 hours and 30 minutes, because the race isn't held at that distance anymore. This record is held by the amazing endurance athlete, Mimi Anderson. Mimi has one of the most impressive athletic CVs I have ever seen, with Guinness World Records under her name. The new, longer, distance record stands at 7 days, 4 hours and 50 minutes, which was set by a Romanian called Tiberiu Useriu in 2018, the first edition of the new distance. Both Jonny and I believe this is definitely beatable. There is only a 31-mile difference between the two distances, but 29 hours and 30 minutes between the two records; this stimulates my mathematical brain. Another question raised its inquisitive head whilst thinking about the records. What if someone finished the new distance in a quicker time than the record of Mimi's on the 352 miler? Would that mean there was then only one record? Jonny lifted my spirits and has now become a good friend and a brilliant training partner, along with his younger brother Conner who is also very athletic. He works in the armed forces and is always up for whatever crazy training exercise we can come up with. I found this out when I accompanied him on a training weekend over the Brecon Beacons in south Wales where, for some reason, trodden paths didn't apply. Whatever direction the compass said, that was the way we went, regardless of the terrain. It could be swamp land, rivers, marsh or forest. If that's the way the compass said, that's the way we were going.

Training in February continued pretty much to plan, slightly short on mileage, but plenty of circuits and strength training: motivation, confidence and, most importantly, enthusiasm, for the miles were building.

March

Adding a further 25 miles in March and taking the required total for the month to 175 miles, started to feel difficult, but not for the reason I would have guessed. The new problem was finding the time to actually fit the training into a weekly schedule of running a gym, performing 40 plus personal training sessions a week, and spending quality time at home with Teri and the girls. With the additional circuits and weights to help build endurance and resilience bolted onto the mileage, this was already very much becoming a juggling act. Five and a half miles average per day for the month doesn't sound too taxing when you consider my target of 60 miles per day was needed on the 6633, but I was starting to feel it. Miss a day because of other daily duties and the distance doubles and then triples. I really don't like playing catch up, and it didn't take much before the accumulation required a 20-mile day to get back on track.

Everything was going swimmingly until March 23rd when the whole of the country, along with most of the first world, went arse over tit and was switched off. The Covid19 Lockdown was announced with instant effect, and I had to lock the doors of the club and stay at home. What a slap around the face. I had only just spent thousands of borrowed monies on the maintenance, as well as the rebuild and to fully stock a functional gym. The club membership had reached the point where it, in the words of a good friend, "started wiping its own backside", i.e., covering its own bills. Then I was told, along with most other businesses, I had to shut down. Ouch!

This stage in my coaching career had taken six years to reach, and I had every penny I could borrow riding on it. How could I expect to keep the already-established members if I couldn't offer them a place to exercise or receive help? The only alternative I could offer was daily virtual circuit classes, which I performed in our home in the family front room. For an hour a day I was in front of the camera performing a circuit class and praying enough members would join me. This would then give the membership a small value, hopefully helping with damage limitation. I have so much respect for the members: the damage to the club, after being closed for over three months, was minimal, and this comes down to the amazing community we have in the club.

April

Well, April 2020; what can I say? Covid, again. You're probably sick of hearing about it, but it was such a massive year. Everything came to a full stop globally. The pandemic that changed everything; but what it was going to change everything into was anybody's guess. Everyone was forced to stay home, with one of the only exceptions being that we were allowed to take one hour's exercise per day. This could be cycling, walking or running (no stationary exercise like circuits, football or tennis, etc). You could also leave the house for food shopping as long as it was only one designated house member. All businesses closed apart from key companies, i.e., food, health, hygiene and medical.

The circuit classes for members continued and were live-streamed. We did a different circuit every day for near-on one hundred days which did three things: 1) it maintained my focus on the business and the amazing community we had built; 2) the bodyweight circuits actually and unexpectedly improved my fitness and flexibility...it was always bodyweight classes because very few people had any gym equipment at home; 3) it helped towards members' continued support and was an important factor in maintaining membership contributions. So, lots of variations in exercises, accompanied by a good hour or so on my feet every day added up to a comfortable 204 miles for the month, along with a fit and productive body.

My low periods came back in the first few weeks of lockdown, and I found on numerous occasions my anxiety attacks returned. After the usual heart-to-hearts with Teri (she puts up with so much from me), the strangest thing happened: I had time. I'd never had time before. What do I do with it? I started to see it as a gift. I grabbed lockdown by the horns and ran with it. During those three months of lockdown, I learned some extremely important lessons. I learned how to relax, how to procrastinate a little, and I learned patience and contentment. I learned the value in the small things; and the most important lesson was just to be comfortable with 'being'.

I had been working too hard for too long. Seventy-hour weeks were the norm, with 50 of these hours giving energy to clients and feeding them with positivity, encouragement and support, so they could be as healthy and as happy as me. This, of course, was mostly a big fat lie; I was emotionally knackered. I faked my way through the day, helping and guiding clients to a healthier, more balanced and productive life, which I wasn't living myself. I was starting to feel like a bit of a fraud. The lockdown forced a full stop to this roller coaster and let me take a breath. This breath came in the form of walking; every day I just walked. I recentred, refocused, reinvented my future, and developed different goals. I had spent so many years fighting for financial success and security; I had used so much of my time chasing the pound, that I think I lost the reason why I wanted the pound in the first place. The strangest thing was that I had already reached a level of success higher than I thought possible four years earlier, but I felt obliged to fight for more. I am by no means wealthy; I just didn't want to feel the stress anymore that coincides with the questions: what if the car stops? What if the oven breaks? How can I afford Christmas this year? Having time to think whilst strolling through field after field corrected this urge to chase the pound, and just made me feel content with what I had.

Whilst digesting this revelation and reinventing myself, another thought inquisitively hovered around my slightly meditative state. This thought turned into a voice that continued to whisper in my ear, "What was I actually capable of?" If I really, and I mean truly, tried, what was my max? Just once, if I give something my everything, what could I do?

May

This whispering continued teasing me into May. As lockdown slowly lifted a little at a time, it became easier, and thoroughly enjoyable, as I covered mile after mile. We were conveniently in the middle of probably the best heatwave I can remember in the UK. Ten weeks of 25 to 30 degrees sunshine. It was just bliss to lose myself for hours at a time. The live circuit feeds continued daily throughout the whole month and developed into a great habit and focus for the clients and for me.

That one question was still reverberating around my little head though, "What was I truly capable of?" I have failed a lot of races and events. Some I've failed through poor nutrition, some through poor hydration, some through wrong clothing or equipment choices, some unbalanced electrolytes, and some I just needed to fail because of the lack of training and the search for suffering.

But when it comes down to it, mostly because of ego, I believed I was good enough, strong enough and stubborn enough to power through anything. Even some of my successes have been failures. I didn't learn from the unnecessary struggle each of the events brought on me. I just wore the struggle, the injury, and the hardship like a badge of pride for everyone to see, so that, in my eyes, they would stand in awe at my achievement. This, of course, did one thing... feed my ego and encourage it to grow more needy and powerful. Most, if not all my finishes were achieved through grit, determination, ego and stubbornness. I was never sufficiently trained, prepared, properly clothed, ate the best foods, kept suitably hydrated, or even considered the actual race as anything worth worrying about. I would just rock up, do the best I could in the quickest time I could manage, struggle through the whole event, totally hate it and totally hate myself for being underprepared, then just see what the result was.

I'm surprised I even signed up for another challenge, but my ego needed continuous stimulation, with a new enthusiasm for a new challenge, and with the promise to myself that I would do better. I would let myself perform in exactly the same way; just rock up, fingers crossed. Trying to finish a challenge with stubbornness and ego was a total failure, regardless of the conclusion. The end result was insignificant. I'd learnt absolutely nothing. Not only was I failing at failure, but I was also failing at success too. This had to change.

June

As the miles and hours grew, so did the time in my sometimes-over-enthusiastic head. I started dreaming and contemplating. Maybe I could become a contestant and not just a participant; maybe I could strive for the gold. Is being a contestant something I am capable of if I gave something my all? Am I actually capable of winning this race? What would it mean? Could it be the start of a new chapter if I won? How much extra training would it take? The questions were endless, resulting in answers that built up a fire, a belief and an energy that inevitably led to answering the biggest, and the first question of the day... "COULD I WIN THIS...YES, I BLOODY COULD".

It came to me like an epiphany. The 6633 Ultra was the answer. I didn't want to turn up just to participate with fingers crossed and hope I'd trained enough to warrant a finish. I wanted the end result to be a formality. Believing that, if I worked harder, trained longer, covered more miles, practised over and over again every skill set needed for this race - I mean three or four times more than anyone else in the race - then not just finishing, but winning would just be the lap of honour.

I started to understand that the race had already started; it started the day I signed up back in January. From that day I was competing with everyone else. It's just the way things are and have always been. Whoever puts in the most effort gets the best results in anything in life. So, after answering the first big question, "could I win this", then the next question came along, "was I doing enough?"

Was I getting up earlier, was I covering more miles, was I practising the housekeeping and maintaining my physicality better than anyone else? Was I managing nutrition and hydration better than anyone else? Did I spend more time researching equipment and was I doing more in regard to acclimatisation than everyone else? Becoming so comfortable with discomfort, that discomfort itself became normal. So many processes and ideas formed in June, and it was like a snowball effect; it became a habit to look for discomfort. I was starting to become obsessed.

July

With this new-found drive of actually being a contender, my imagination and enthusiasm grew exponentially with each day on the tarmac. I devised a six-month training programme, which would include hundreds of bodyweight exercises every week. These would include press ups, sit ups, pull ups and weighted squats; a daily stretching routine, breathing exercises, meditation, ice baths, and of course, a ridiculous number of miles. All this was to prevent injury and to build strength and endurance. I understand that to train for a 383-mile race, to finish in less than seven days to break the record and do it in arctic conditions, you have to do more than just practise covering a lot of miles. That's only the piece of the iceberg you can see. The other 80% of the iceberg you can't see is building a body that can cope with not only the mileage, but also the 3,830 miles needed during training to be a contender. I would need powerful, dense, low-weight muscle to hold the skeleton together. I would need a strong, secure back, capable of pulling a 60Ib sled for seven days. I would need the flexibility in my joints to overcome any unforeseen twists or misplaced feet when muscle fatigue has set in. The ability to withstand and perform in extreme conditions is a priority; if you can't get your gloves on because your hands are too cold, it's game over. Even the nutrition needed training; firstly, to let your digestion learn how to acquire the most nutrition out of a new food source, and secondly, just to see what was still edible at -20 degrees Celsius. These, and many other scenarios and ideas needed rolling over, answering, practising and learning. Bit by bit I would add new objectives to my monthly training.

This was my plan for the next six months:

August was to include some 20 plus mile hikes and the introduction of additional bodyweight exercises to strengthen the core, legs and back. 500 press-ups, 500 sit-ups, 250 weighted squats and 250 pull ups every week for the entirety of the training.

September introduced one of my old fears - the dark. I would need to include 10pm or 3am 20-mile stints every couple of weeks. Those demons needed overcoming because over 50% of the race is in the dark. Also, the big test for September would be my 100 miles in one-day challenge, to see if I was learning and progressing, and to eventually put to bed this haunting nemesis: more on this later.

October: The mileage would be stepped up again. This month 350 miles would be on the table, including, on at least two occasions, a 30-plus-mile hike with half the time in the dark, practising the routine I would use in Canada, which is to walk in 4 hour blocks with 20 minute breaks between each, hopefully linking four blocks together each day: 17 hours of work and 7 hours for recovery and maintenance.

November's programme would be much the same but stepping it up to a couple of days of 3 blocks of 4 hours. I would start investigating and include the nutritional options available, while still maintaining plenty of bodyweight, heavy lifting and circuit training.

Two full 4 block days would be included in December. The mileage expected on these days would hopefully hover around 60 miles. This is the average day's distance needed if I am going to finish in less than 7 days.

January: the last and biggest month of training. 425 miles needed to go onto the Garmin, including two full days of walking, and overnight sleeps in the bivvy bag. Four blocks on the Saturday, 4 hours sleep, 2 blocks on the Sunday – 100-mile weekends - eating as I would be eating and cooking as I would cooking. On the alternate weekends, introducing pulling of the sled for 30 miles at a time. Such a massive month planned. February was all about practise, practise and practise: every scenario possible from climbing in and out of the sleeping bag as quickly as possible and cooking food on my stove, to eating arctic foods most nights in the dark. I needed to know the whereabouts of every single item in my possession. If it didn't serve a purpose, it didn't come. I wanted to feel comfortable with every situation; even going for poos outside needed to become routine. Yes, July was definitely the month it all came together. The mind switched and it became an addiction. I was focused - time to put this plan into action.

August

Here we go! Six months of dedication, resilience, discomfort and adaptation. The target for this month was 300 miles and I managed to squeeze in an extra one point two miles. I say squeezed in; I was holding myself back from over-performing. There is always the danger of peaking too early. A steady, organised increase in training is just as much for the mind as it is for the body. The mind, after all, is what makes you finish a race, not the body. The incremental increase during training also escalates the hunger and stretches the resilience in the mind. Feed the hunger too early and you lose the need to finish. The mental switch in July was powerful; this was now my way of life. Three hundred miles wasn't hard at all. I was exercising more, bouncing out of bed in the early hours, taking daily cold showers, nutrition and hydration were on point; I was sleeping like a baby, and surprisingly needed less sleep. Any spare time was used researching equipment, reading previous participants' blogs, and visualising different points of the race as to how I would deal with similar issues. I felt good, powerful and strong - I was ready.

It was on the 14th of August that I had the dream about documenting this growth. The first words of this book were typed on the 15th of August, and by the end of the month twenty thousand words were already being manipulated into a story. So now, adding to my monthly mileage that was close to warranting a road tax charge for my feet, along with the endless exercise, practising, researching, coaching, business duties and family time, I needed to write a book. Why not? I did say I wanted more.

August flew by. I didn't even know what day it was most of the time. Every minute was occupied. Days became longer with 5am starts and 10pm finishes. Day by day I was becoming stronger, deeper and more focused. I was looking forward to September so that I could lift my game a bit more and venture into more discomfort, thus allowing me to grow further.

September

At the start of the month, I was on fire; anything to create discomfort. I would wake up at random times just to walk for three miles because I didn't want to. Cold showers and baths became the norm because I didn't want to. I increased my training to a couple of times a day because the first one wasn't uncomfortable enough. My self-belief was growing, accepting that winning could just be a formality.

Growing self-belief is a powerful asset. It's not something anyone or anything can give you. It's similar to developing and keeping a fit, healthy, strong body: there are no shortcuts, no magic pills or potions, and no secret recipes. You can't buy, steal or inherit it, and it can't be held onto without constant dedicated, and repetitive hard work. Self-belief is built up with the same devotion and discipline, living under the same roof. Once you have it, it can take you places you never knew existed. But it can be rocked, and when it does, the fall can be very painful. It's hard enough to establish it the first time, but when you've been knocked off the pedestal, getting back on can sometimes be impossible.

On the 7th of September, I was rocked. It came in the form of an email, and this email stood at the base of my pedestal and shook me off.

The 2021 edition of the 6633 Arctic Ultra had been cancelled. SHIT!

Mileage

Jan 2020	125	124
Feb 2020	150	142.4
March 2020	175	174.4
April 2020	200	204.8
May 2020	225	223.5
June 2020	250	245.8
July 2020	275	271.8
August 2020	300	301.2

Chapter 11
The E-mail

Deep down I knew it was coming, but wishfully hoping I would be wrong, and we'd escape the same fate as so many other races and events this year. Everything after March 23rd had come to a full stop, and slowly but surely the cancellation of events was creeping closer to the end of the year. Nothing was allowed to take place in October; then November, and then December - would the tidal wave stop before hitting us? With the news that two other events in Whitehorse had already been given the red light at the end of August, we were all just waiting for our phones to ping with an email giving us the inevitable news.

Early morning on the 7th of September it came, and even though I was expecting it, I still sat at the kitchen table in disbelief, re-reading the whole message four or five times looking for a glimmer of hope; hoping that it was just a warning, and that if things go our way, there could still be a chance we could go. But no - every time I read it, the words were exactly the same. The unarguable answer was, 'it's not happening this year'. Covid had struck again.

The email had been sent from Martin, who - you could tell by the way it read - was distraught about the decision he was forced to make. A big part of me felt for him. I knew he wanted it as much as we did, and I'm sure he tried his absolute best to make it happen. The main reasons for the decision were, firstly, Canada was still closed to everyone. It might change before the skiing season, but why take the chance? The border crossings were shut, apart from the emergency services between the Yukon and the Northern Territories which we must cross 60 miles into the race. Secondly, the local small communities with populations of only a few hundred pleaded with visitors to stay away from fear of Covid arriving. Most of the communities were terrified; the only interaction they had had with the pandemic was the misguided information they heard on news feeds and social media. Lastly, the Coast High Country Inn in Whitehorse, which was always used in the previous years for the official meeting point for all competitors, had been taken over by local officials as an isolation unit for travellers in and out of the territory. It was still 24 weeks until we were to arrive, and things could very possibly change, but with the threat of a second wave, I wouldn't put any of my hard-earned money on it. So, with a clear understanding of the training needed, and the financial commitment for a challenge like this, Martin stepped up and made the exceedingly difficult decision.

Physically gutted and mentally numb, I sat at the kitchen table for over an hour, staring out the patio doors into our ungroomed, neglected garden. The biggest thing on my mind was then overshadowed by how many other things I had neglected, along with people in my life while preparing for this event. Every night I would close my eyes thinking about the 6633; I woke up in the early hours thinking of the 6633. I had already given nearly nine months of training to it. I'd manufactured a fourteen-month training program and was sticking to it religiously for the first time (surprise, surprise)! I was already buying equipment, raising money for the NHS, sampling frozen foods straight from the freezer, building an inquisitive following, and even writing this book with whatever spare time I had, hoping I would have the majority of it finished before flying to Canada.

Then, whilst in Canada creating the romantic conclusion I needed for the book, winning it. What now?

Someone had just told the six-year-old me that Christmas isn't happening. Believe it or not, my saviour was in fact this book.

Other disappointments throughout my short forty-seven years have slowly built an understanding of the process I go through before I can look at things logically, reassess, then make a new plan before moving forward.

I was given similar unfortunate news in 2013 when the Black Ice Race was cancelled a few weeks before departure. I hit the floor hard after receiving that email, too. It took weeks to go through the usual set of emotions most people go through when they've been rejected or lost something. Weeks went by before I was able to pick myself back up and move forward. First came the disbelief which lasted a few days. Then came the anger; I wasn't nice to be around. I argued with whomever, about whatever I could; any opportunity to release the pain. I even took a week off work. I couldn't be bothered with all the mundane daily living activities, problems and the pettiness surrounding them. I would be infuriated at how petty people could seriously be about some idiot who had been voted off Britain's Got Talent the night before, saying to myself, as I witnessed their frustration, "do you bloody know what I am going through?" Thinking how bloody ridiculous their lives must be if their favourite act on Britain's Got Talent getting voted off is the worst thing that's happening to them. I thought it best to stay away from people before I either got fired from work or punched someone. This lasted for a few days before convincing myself there was a compromise. I could find and register for a different race. I would feel a whole lot better if I developed a new relationship with a different, equally stupid, adventure: technically a rebound relationship, and we all know how they work out. A rebound race never works, but, just the same, I did it anyway, which, as you know, was my first visit to the 6633 in 2013. It didn't help. I fell into a depressive state for a couple of weeks before accepting it for what it was, and just moved forward.

Looking through the patio doors after the fifth read of the email, and the disbelief now turning to belief, I could feel anger brewing. Who was I angry with? Martin? It wasn't his fault. Covid? I suppose a bit, but thousands of people were suffering more than this. Fate? Things happen for a reason... am I self-centred enough to believe that this whole global pandemic happened to stop me from going to Canada? I had nothing and nobody to be angry with. This was when I realised that I was already starting the usual process of loss, so why fight it. If this was the case, let's reduce the collateral damage, I thought. So, I retreated upstairs to the bedroom, closely followed by Teri to show support and a shoulder. She was swiftly turned away and told to leave me alone. I then spent the next couple of hours bouncing off the walls, becoming angry at inanimate objects, and aggravated with myself for not finishing the paintwork in the en-suite. It was time to force a different outcome, so I took a breath, then a step, and then, finally, found myself one minute later, out the front door and heading for an eight-mile run, something I totally didn't want to do. What was the point? There was no bloody race, after all. But I did, and it was one of the fastest eight miles I had ever run, with an average heart rate of 171 beats. I never sustain that intensity of a heart rate. The run worked though, I returned with an idea... "let's find a new race". I did; it was the John O' Groats to Lands' End challenge, set at the same time in March; An 860-mile multistage race over 17 days. Spot on, perfect; that'll tick the box, that's just what I needed. Just before clicking the purchase button on their website, a virtual slap reminded me that rebound races don't work.

It's not going to help, and I'll probably fail so, disappointedly, I switched off the computer, but at least I saved the £3000 entry fee and a right old telling off from Teri.

With that, and knowing I shouldn't even try entering anything else, I grew more depressed as the day, and then the night, went on. Spending most of the next 14 hours slipping in and out of sleep, I needed a release. I needed the waterworks. I needed this last stage of the process so I could come back to sanity, but I couldn't let the tears out. Halfway through Sunday afternoon, still in bed, I looked into the side drawer and found the three letters given to me from Teri and the girls; the three I took to the Arctic. These heartfelt words of encouragement were always exactly what I needed, always hitting the spot. Seconds later the floodgates opened. Hearing me sobbing from downstairs, Teri came up to console me, and as I rested my heavy head onto her legs as she sat upright on the bed, I drifted contentedly away. Waking up an hour later, and ready to reassess, I was ready to make a new plan and move forward.

What took weeks in 2013, took 36 hours this time. I was learning from my own book as I was writing it: "Don't fail at failure". I took my own advice. The cancellation of the 2021 race wasn't my failure, but how I dealt with it could have been.

The revelation of the book came from a dream I had one Saturday morning at the beginning of August, a few weeks earlier. I dreamt I had already written a book - this book - the one you are reading. I was travelling around the country selling it at functions, events and village halls. A few copies here, a few there, making steady sales. I would do motivational talks in businesses, sporting events and running clubs, building a nice head of steam with its popularity. But every now and then a potential customer would ask me something about a specific part of the story. "How did you deal with that?"; "Where do you find your inspiration from?"; "How did Teri take that?" The problem was that I didn't have any answers. I shockingly became aware I had no idea what the book was about so, continuing within the dream, I grabbed a coffee and a chair, sat down and got stuck into my own book: reading the whole thing in one sitting. I was so impressed with what I had written that it woke me up. I jumped out of bed in the dark hours of the morning and wrote a two-thousand-word synopsis of the entire thing: the name of the book, chapter subjects, chapter headings, storylines - everything. Five weeks later, as the email rocked my weekend, I'd already laid down thousands of words, but it needed an ending. The email had taken that away. Now, totally engrossed in finishing the book, the answer was clear. I knew how this would end, and I now know the postponement of the race was probably for the best.

Time to make a new plan...

This hasn't been the only event cancelled during this historic year. Many a race has succumbed to a virtual version of its event. Basically, a virtual event is to give participants a conclusion to his or her hard work and preparations. For a few pounds you could still take part, kind of, by sending the event organiser your recorded distance and time taken whilst running, cycling, or swimming around your local area. In return, you'll be added to the results along with everyone else's times to eventually find the virtual winner. Then you'll receive a t-shirt and a medal as you would any other race. Following the current trend, Martin arranged a virtual 6633. A simple plan. At one minute past midnight on the 1st of March 2021, the clock starts and continues to tick until 383 miles have been proven completed. Trophies would be given for the first and second fastest finishers during an award party on the 31st of March. This was open for all previous and current participants, along with anyone who fancied a ridiculously long challenge. After considering the options, I soon realised the virtual 6633 could benefit me greatly. Firstly, my nine months of training wouldn't go to waste. It's mentally painful to train for anything so hard, and then have the conclusion taken away. You build a head of steam, an energy that needs a release, and without the expected release, you create a new mindset, built on a foundation of frustration. You then have a house full of anger, stress, anxiety and depression. In other words, you become a very unhappy bunny. So, my training programme would still fit - roughly. I wouldn't necessarily need to train for the same weather conditions, although covering 383 miles with the temperature between -20 and -50 degrees Celsius, along with the snow and high winds, sounds more attractive than the possibility of hiking the same distance for six to nine days in typical early March English weather. This could very realistically be heavy rain, high winds, grey skies and possible damp snow. I hate performing in waterproofs; you're either wet from the rain or wet from the sweat. Martin set the rule of completing the distance during the month of March as quickly as possible. I decided to complete the race as close to the original as I could, with the same rules. 383 miles needed on the clock within the nine days, pulling my sled for the entirety of the challenge around Lutterworth, sleeping outside or in my van each night, eating the same foods that would be available at -20 degrees Celsius, and only allowing myself hot-and-cold-water refills at the same checkpoint miles as in Canada.

Another, and possibly the main reason this new plan made me excited, was the opportunity to develop a massive local awareness of my adventures. Witnessing some idiot dragging a blue sled on wheels around the streets of Lutterworth would make the local community very inquisitive.

Great for the charity, great for business, great for social media followers, and great for building that much-needed support for the 2022 race. I know it sounds a bit vain to be worried about social media, but I am going to be selling a book soon.

Lastly, it makes a great twist in the book, and creates an opportunity for a second book. The romantic conclusion of this first book will obviously finish with the completion of the virtual, in style. But there will still be a big part of the story left to tell - revisiting Canada in 2022. This, along with returning to some of my DNF's already mentioned, i.e. The 100-mile South Downs, the 100-mile North Downs, and The Race to the Stones 100 km, will make the 12 months between March 2021 and March 2022 a massive year for rectifying my past naivety, and the perfect opportunity to show I have read and digested my own book.

Decision made, challenge set, and training can continue as planned, but with a few adjustments. Now, with three additional events on the radar, the ratio of miles during training, between the jogging miles and the walking miles, would need to change. The trilogy of events added to the calendar during the summer is only separated by four weeks each, the SDW100 in June, the Race to the Stones 100km in July, and the NDW100 in August. These are also running events, not walking, especially if I wanted to continue to be competitive. When I say competitive, I am realistic. These events are a totally different ball game. I do believe some genetic help is required to win these types of events. There are some things that just can't be done; you can't beat genetics. I know it's impossible for me to run a sub-2-hour 30-minute marathon. It doesn't matter how much I trained; it wasn't possible; I wasn't built that way. I carry too much weight; I don't have the lungs for it, and I don't have legs up to my armpits. A victory for me in the summer races would be finishing in the top 10%. For a 48-year-old without the genetic gifts for running, to finish in the top 20 finishers would make me smile like the proverbial Cheshire cat. A possible sub-

19-hour finish would still be required for the 100-miles. With only a 12-week gap between the chequered flag of the virtual 6633 and the starting gun of the SDW100, and then only four weeks separating each of the summer events. I would have to train for all the events at the same time, making sure I was able to repair and rebuild between them efficiently.

First things first, though. I was only days away from our Club's 24-hour challenge, and an opportunity to prove I can complete 100 miles in one day.

Chapter 12
The Morning After

The morning after used to mean a hangover; lots of coffee and anything edible, as long as it was greasy. A vague memory of the night before, hoping I hadn't made a complete idiot of myself, and a banging headache. Today's morning after left a totally different impression, still needing a shot or two of caffeine and the urge to eat like a horse, but this time I remembered every second of the previous day. It was the morning after a 24-hour endurance challenge, organised and run from my very own SB Health and Fitness club.

This event materialised months before because, as a club, we had two separate four person teams and one solo runner (I was the solo) entered an official race called the Equinox 24. The objective of the race is to run, jog, walk or crawl as many laps as possible of a 10 km route in 24 hours. This can be done as a solo runner, in a pair completing alternate laps, or in a team with one person out on the track at any given time. As with everything else in 2020, it was cancelled. This was going to be one of the highlights of the club's year and, I believe, something everyone involved needed. It was something to look forward to away from the difficulties surrounding us all this year. Sylvia came up with the idea, or a moment of madness, depending on how you look at it, of running an event at the club around the same rules on the same day. Word spread in the club and, not only did it lift everyone's heads again, but it also attracted a few more willing participants, creating an additional two teams of four people to join in.

With weeks and months of training in the bag, September the 19th got crossed off the calendar. I was excitedly nervous and arrived at the club just before 8.30am. There was already a hustle of preparations taking place, as people found their own little space in the world for the next 24 hours. The atmosphere was electric, continuing to build whenever another team-mate walked through the doors. Everyone brought their own luxuries in the hope it would ease, even slightly, any discomfort during whatever lay ahead. Sleep mats, sleeping bags, duvets, pillows; even a large garden lounger came through the door along with everyone's favourite foods and treats. We had lasagne, curries, casseroles, hot dogs, chocolate cakes, crumbles, biscuits and energy drinks; the variety was endless. I couldn't wait to get stuck in, but knew I had to earn it first. Besides, I don't think running with a huge bowl of apple crumble in my belly at ten in the morning would be a good way to start a 100-mile challenge, as much as I wanted to.

All the athletes were present and accounted for by 9.30, so it was time for a quick chat to re-establish the rules and to go over the health and safety points before the local newspaper dropped in for a story and a few photos. Those 15 minutes, fortunately, calmed the tension and anticipation for most of them; but for me, it was another obstacle before I could focus on the task at hand. Ten minutes left, and as the photographer was taking the last couple of photos, my anxiety started increasing. I still needed to Vasoline my feet, chest, as well as - mind your own business! For quick turnarounds between laps, I still needed to triple-check that everything was where I thought it was. I still needed to decide which hat to wear and whether my shoelaces were at the correct tension.

At last, the local newspaper had done their bit, and with all my final adjustments taken care of, it was my turn to count down. 5, 4, 3, - everyone's fingers hovering over the side buttons on their sports watches to make sure the miles were counted - 2 and 1. We were off, for the first lap of the four-and-a-half-mile loop around Lutterworth. We turned right as we exited the car park, headed straight for half a mile along the busiest road in town, continually looking out for a space in the traffic to cross, knowing that to prevent us from departing Lutterworth, we would need to turn left. From this 90-degree corner there's a long sweeping, consistently declining turn of 90 degrees to the left, which lasts a further half a mile before reaching a small painted roundabout where we turned right along an undulating road for exactly a mile, past the entrance to my home where my daughters were probably only just waking up to an empty house, joyfully remembering they have the place to themselves for the day. At a brand-new, larger roundabout, built only months previously because of a recent housing development, which took away one of my favourite cross-country routes, I might add, we turned left. Heading towards the centre of town, past the Red Arrow Pub on the right and the town park on the left next to the leisure centre, we totted up another three-quarters of a mile before nearly turning back on ourselves with a sharp left at the war memorial. This would then lead back to the main busy road, via the little painted roundabout, to where we originally turned left half a mile from the club. It wasn't long before we re-entered the car park from where we had started, to a welcoming cheer from all the others waiting in anticipation for team members to reappear. Lap 1 completed for me in 40 minutes flat, 2 minutes ahead of plan.

This challenge became more than a fun escapade with friends to provide a conclusion to the months of training for them and for myself; this was to be the proof I needed that I was starting to grow, learn, adapt and evolve from my previous lessons learnt as an ultra-runner. I had attempted one hundred miles five times in previous years. The first and only successful finish was the already-mentioned Grim Reaper. Similar to our event, it loops for 10 miles around the picturesque grounds of Grimsthorpe Castle in the south of Lincolnshire, with three options available for the athletes: four laps, seven laps or ten laps, all within a 26-hour time limit. We know by now that I jumped in at the deep end. My mathematical logic provided the answer. One hundred miles divided by 26 hours equals a comfortable 3.85 mph, or 15.58-minute miles. I can do that. I knew I could hold 10-minute miles / 6 mph for half a marathon, and I knew I could walk at an average 4 mph / 15-minute miles because I had done that on the Just Walk event for 60 km's the year before. All I had to do was keep moving; just keep placing one step in front of the other - easy. That was settled then; I picked the 100 miles. With three friends joining me on the Grim Reaper, two of them, Andy and Mikey, wisely went for the 40-mile option. On the other hand, Gyula, with his eyes also bigger than his belly, was as optimistic or as stupid as me, went for the 10 laps. Andy was a new addition to our party whom I had coerced into my carryings-on. He worked as a team leader in the same team as Mikey and me. He has an amazing supportive personality; taller and a little younger than me with an infectious smile. He had only just felt the addiction of running and had recently finished his first half marathon, so he was eager to join another challenge. We all signed up and proceeded with trying to raise some money. After all, this was the reason I was looking for something extraordinary.

I figure that the best way to see how I had developed over the years was to compare the two events, and how I felt during and after each one. The reason behind the first 100-mile attempt was to raise some much-needed funds to help a local mother and daughter. The daughter was called Megan who, through a very unfair dealing of the cards, had been told she'd developed a brain tumour, and this was before her third birthday. She had attended the local nursery where my daughters had started their schooling years but was then moved to a local hospice for children called Rainbows. Hearing this news affected me and all I wanted to do was help. The only strengths I had were my work ethic and my stubbornness, and the only help I could think of was to make her last days as interesting and as comfortable as possible. Therefore, I spent a couple of days trawling the internet for something that sounded menacing enough to encourage people to put their hands in their pockets and show support. The 100-mile Grim Reaper sounded intimidating and ridiculous enough to raise some eyebrows. With some very generous donations we accumulated £2,600, so job one done. Job two, training; a couple of 30-mile walkie/jogs in the bank and we were setting up tents in the gardens of Grimsthorpe Castle the night before job three, my first attempt at 100 miles in one day - something that from the outside looked totally Olympian, considering that running a marathon would normally be the biggest talking point for months amongst the people I circled with day to day.

This was also my first experience of an ultra-event. I had participated in a few 10 km races and a couple of half marathons, but this was different. The atmosphere surprised me. There wasn't the usual hustling and last-minute preparations, as athletes scurried around in their unique little worlds. This was social, even slightly calming, as competitors communicated through respect and admiration of each other, sharing stories of past victories and war wounds over a warm beverage. As I sat on my 18-inch-high foldable stool whilst Mikey and Andy prepared their meal for the evening, and with Gyula currently tucking into his, I drifted into tomorrow. Had I set myself too much? How much pain was I going to feel? How emotional was the finish going to feel? I had never run nor walked through the night before. It's a strange feeling knowing you're expecting to skip a night's sleep the next day, just for the fun of it.

All the tents stood on soft, well-groomed grass between a very well-established tree line and the finish/start track, which led up to the magnificent four-meter-high cast iron gates of the stately home. With the sun already set and the haunting darkness surrounding us, Grimsthorpe Castle stood proudly at the top of the hill, illuminated from every angle, giving the impression you were in the presence of greatness. The dominance of this Disney-esq building would demand the attention of our glazed eyes as I imagined its welcoming splendour on the completion of each lap during the event the next day.

This was, in truth, only my third attempt at camping, and I hated sleeping bags. I fidget when asleep; being imprisoned in a cocoon never encouraged a relaxed night's sleep, so I didn't get much shuteye.

Nevertheless, the next moment my eyes opened it was race day and, still with an unexpected calmness, 200 runners ate their huge breakfast, taped up their calves and hamstrings, and donned a spectacular variety of colourful lycra in the form of tights, shorts, leggings, vests and t-shirts. An amazing selection of running equipment accompanied each runner. Some preferred hip bags, some had strangely shaped rucksacks that held water bottles on the front near their chests, and others preferred a multitude of pockets to carry energy gels and cereal bars whilst carrying a specially shaped water bottle for ease of grip. I preferred my two-litre bladder, carried in a small camelback rucksack which I'd just managed to fill before we slowly manoeuvred between two brick pillows standing menacingly on the right side of the castle. This is where, at 9.30, the gun would echo through the tranquil English countryside to start our first revolution of these outstanding grounds. The current owner Jane Heathcote-Drummond-Willoughby, 28th Baroness Willoughby de Eresby, had the responsibility to maintain and protect Grimsthorpe Castle in its entirety, and she was obviously proud of her work.

Boxed together in this relatively small space between the pillars, Mikey looked up with fear in his eyes and said, "I think we've forgotten something". "What"? I replied in a panic. "We forgot to train," he said. As we all burst out laughing, the gun fired.

Back in Lutterworth, I was heading out on my fourth Lap. The first three went well, all returning a 40-minute lap time, and creating a 12-minute lead on my planned schedule. The objective of the day wasn't necessarily to race, but to use it as a training exercise to see if I had the distance in me without injury. I needed to see if my learnings were working, and it was looking good so far. But then the sun hit the very peak of the sky, sending the mercury rising. Between the fourth and ninth rotations, all I could do was to drink; any thought of nutrition just churned my stomach. I wasn't coping with the heat at all, but with encouragement from other SB Health & Fitness family members along the route, shouting out support and smashing out the high fives, I battled through. I do believe I swallowed over six litres of water before the sunset on the eleventh lap without once needing to use the toilet once, well apart from a chronic case of diarrhoea on the fifth lap, which sent me, cheeks clenched, shuffling into my home halfway round. This was the exact same situation that happened on the Grim Reaper.

It was the final quarter of a mile on the third lap of the Grim Reaper, just as the start-finish tent came into view at the top of the hill, when an unexpected bowel movement occurred, once again needing a clenched shuffle to save myself. It's such a distinctive jog when you're clenching. You run from the knees down making everyone aware of the battle you are facing. The culprit again was the heat. I remember filling my two-litre bladder, each time from empty, as I completed every one of the first six laps, which translates to 60 miles, 17 hours and 12 litres of water without the need for relief.

Towards the end of my fourth lap, I saw a familiar body shape upfront; it was Mikey, with Andy not too far ahead. They both looked as bad as I felt, battle-scarred from nearly forty miles on underprepared limbs in the continuous unrelenting heat, and clearly dehydrated. After joining them for a few moments and sharing a few quick words, along the lines of, "I really don't care for the sun today" - something like that, anyway - I jogged on. Each ten-mile loop would be celebrated by a visit to my little two-man tent for a refill, and maybe to indulge in a few calories if my stomach would allow it.

Staggering towards my small home for the fifth time, it quickly became apparent that I didn't bend anymore; my hips to my feet were rigid. With the help of a nearby tree, I walked my hands down the trunk, keeping my frame as straight as possible, and before planting my face into the dusty dry hard soil, I dropped and wormed my way along like an army commando, through the zipped doorway, and collapsed halfway in and halfway out the tent. It was then that I got reunited with Andy and Mikey; both chuffed to bits and in obvious pain from finishing their challenge, medal in one hand and tin of beer in the other. Reversing out of the tent and grappling with the tree for support to get vertical again, I asked them if they had seen Gyula. They replied that they'd just seen him off for his fifth lap. As they stared at their already broken, sunburnt, weak friend who obviously didn't have hinges in his legs anymore, they were stunned when I spoke about finishing it. Only 11 hours had passed, and I was already halfway to the finish, which to my calculations meant I had 15 hours left for the second half. I can walk that out I convinced them, so with an unstable hug from each, I checked out for the sixth time.

Fifty miles around Lutterworth and things were looking up. The sun started making its way to Australia, giving a massive and very much appreciated reprieve from the heat. My digestion had started to wake up, an effect of the slightly more sedentary pace. I had been for a pee with another on the way, so hydration was coming back, and I felt encouraged that I wasn't really in too much pain. Other runners started coupling up as darkness set and the head torches came out. Saturday evening in the suburbs of Lutterworth felt very sedentary, and the next 27 miles were the most comfortable of the entire 100. With a pizza, a piece of chocolate cake, a coffee-flavoured protein drink, and a box of Jaffa cakes that were encouraged down with a couple of cups of tea, I drifted into automatic pilot whilst listening to Ross Edgley's audiobook, 'The Art of Resilience'. This is an amazing book about his titanic swim around the coast of the UK. The whole challenge equated to 1,791 miles in 157 days without setting a single foot ashore for the entirety of the expedition.

The chapter Ross was reading, coincidentally, was about pain, describing how ultra-runners seem to be more resilient and comfortable with continuous pain than most. This definitely helped towards my heightened enthusiasm. The darkness was especially heavy that night as there was no moon, and all the streetlights were switched off from midnight until 5.30am. In recent months, the darkness had become my friend, forced on myself by the regular 3.30am starts on my heavy training days. My claustrophobia had all but gone.

It's in the darkest hours you come face to face with yourself. Most people don't like who they meet, but, for the

161

first time, I had now developed a peace with myself. I enjoyed visiting myself occasionally. I now loved the solitude and isolation that accompanied the dark hours. My thoughts became sharper and more direct at night.

I barely remember anything from 50 to 90 miles in the Grim Reaper. The loneliness was something I hadn't expected. I spent many hours in my own head, constantly arguing with Melvin who was naturally using my claustrophobia as his weapon of choice. Apart from catching up with a visually disturbed Gyula halfway around my sixth lap - his fifth - I didn't see another soul. Gyula seemed to have lost half a foot of his normally strong, proud stature, and I could see in his eyes it was game over. He was clearly in a dark place. I really wanted to stay with him, but I was fighting my own battle, so continued.

Wobbling in at 70 miles, Andy saw me, so I spent an extra five minutes with him as he brought me up to date with the goings-on of our team. Mikey had to go home for work commitments early the next day, and Gyula had pulled out after five laps and was now comatose in the tent.

After inhaling my usual rations of the biscuits and tea, Andy walked me out for the first few hundred metres of the next lap and wished me well as I disappeared into the dark blanket of the early hours.

From speaking to Mikey and Andy at the halfway stage, it took me 11 and a half hours to cover another four laps, taking my total to nine laps, with each lap becoming more laboured. I would eat a box of Jaffa cakes and drink two cups of sweet tea on each return.

I always choose these little treats because of their willingness to be dunked, whilst temporarily still holding their rigid construction due to the orange-flavoured chocolate topping, and then loved the ease at which they dissolved once placed into the mouth. Perfect for when you need calories but, because of the stress hormones, you struggle with eating.

It was the final lap; the final 10 miles I remember the most. It took just shy of three and a half hours to drag the two dead weights hanging from my hips around, with the walking poles bending as they reluctantly held my body weight. Tears of despair impaired my vision every single second as I guided my limbs over gravel, grass, hardcore and tarmac. I was eight miles through the lap when, as I turned left up a sharp 20-foot incline and across a small narrow footbridge, I could see a silhouette of a person heading towards me shouting my name. Convincing myself it was a hallucination, I mentally told it to bugger off, returning my concentration to my despondent struggle. The figure drifted closer and closer, repeating, "Stu, Stu - you OK?" It was Andy. He'd walked out to encourage me to hurry. Apparently, I was not only the only person left on the course, but I was the only one left at Grimsthorpe Castle, apart from Gyula, who was packing away our kit, and one solitary race organiser who was sat in his Land Rover next to the small pole which was javelined into the earth. He was waiting for me to check-in for the last time, marking the end of the lap and the completion of my race. This was done by tapping my wristband onto the electric reader, mounted at the top of the pole. The moment that happened, he approached with his hand stretched out in front of him, then, with a firm grip around my limp fingers, a respectful shake of the head and full of disbelief on his face, he said, "Wow, you shouldn't have finished that; I'm impressed". With that, he jumped into his Land Rover and drove off, leaving Andy, Gyula and me alone in the vast grounds of the Castle: the weirdest and most anti-climactic finish to any event.

In Lutterworth I had only nine miles left, just two more laps of my hometown. As I left the club for the twenty-first time, I acknowledged the pain that had subtly crept in through the night whilst being on autopilot. One hundred miles on tarmac bloody hurts and I needed solitude to deal with it, but within a few hundred yards, annoyingly, Sylvia and her husband Mick joined me for the penultimate lap. I tried not to spit my dummy out too far, but they quickly understood to stay away, keeping 30 feet behind me. Approaching the club with one lap to go, everyone was outside clapping. Why were they clapping? I still had four and a half of the most agonising miles left before I deserved anything that would resemble applause. Marching straight through them, I filled my water container, placed two chunks of caramel-filled chocolate into my mouth to melt, and then strode past them on the way back out - again. The whole group limped, dragged, whimpered and yawned after me for the victory lap, looking like a dishevelled caterpillar with broken legs. Once again, the need to accept my pain, in my own way, is how I placed one foot in front of the other for the last time. I just had to maintain a distance from them; I really couldn't cope with the thought of someone even breathing into my space. Once the lap was complete, and as I turned left for the very last time into the yard of the club, it was totally agonising, but overwhelmingly joyful. The dishevelled caterpillar scurried past me with half a mile left so they could welcome my return. The clapping, cheering and whistling was a lot more accepted this time, but once again, I 'marched' straight through the centre of them shouting that I haven't finished yet, I must touch the door. Everyone burst out laughing, remarking how much of an idiot I was, but then took it in turns shouting their praises to me as I leant against the wall next to the entrance of the club. The last to reach me was Teri, and, as I lifted my head and made eye contact, the waterworks started. Not so much for the accomplishment, even though that was drowning me, but for the pain. Teri had achieved her own accomplishments during this challenge, being part of a four-person team relaying the 100-mile race around Lutterworth, she covered 6 of her own laps, achieving a marathon distance in the allotted time.

The few days after both my centuries would dictate, more than anything, whether I had evolved, learnt from failure and progressed.

To this day I stand by my word when I say The Grim Reaper damaged me more than any other challenge, I have put myself through. On returning home after travelling for an hour, I remained sat in the car and called my wife to come out of our family home and assist Gyula in carrying me the last few meters to the door. I was as close to becoming an extra in The Walking Dead as I've ever been. No emotion, no energy, no reaction - just broken: broken mentally, physically and spiritually. It was all I could do to get myself into the downstairs wet room. We had had this installed because of Teri's, now improving, disability. I left a smudge on the wall as I slid agonisingly along it for support. Once standing in the shower area with both hands palming the wall, and my forehead firmly resting against the cold white tiles, as if I were about to be patted down by the police, Teri realised how much trouble I was in. She very quickly understood that the only way my clothes were coming off was with the aid of some scissors. With the last thread of clothing cut off the water was switched on, at which point a scream came from somewhere deep at the realisation that both my bum cheeks were very sore and didn't like the clean, fresh water on them. Along with the numerous blisters on my feet, under my armpits and on my nipples, I had developed two moon-shaped blisters on my bum cheeks, one on each: these had both burst, and the sore flesh underneath stuck onto the opposing sore flesh of the other cheek. This resulted in stretching our marriage vows to the limit. I'm not sure 'in sickness and in health' included kneeling behind your spouse, who had one hundred miles of sweat, blood and urine soaked to their skin, slowly parting the cheeks of their backside to see pink blood-infused-water dribble down the inside of their legs. As I delicately passed through the stages of being cleaned, dried and treated for injuries, I could feel a state of panic developing. Fifteen minutes later I'm on the floor in the foetal position, shaking uncontrollably; eventually passing out for a couple of hours. I then spent the next 24 hours going through a three hour cycle of two hours sleep, a full meal, a quick chat, and back to sleep. Four days passed before I went to the toilet without traces of blood and was able to move freely around the house. This also forced a week off work to recover. Strangely, it was during this week off work that I entered my next Ultra.

This time, in Lutterworth, it proved a different story. Lowering myself onto a gym bench in the club was surprisingly hard but felt unbelievably good to release the weight from my feet. Everyone was still smiling, chirping and competing for air space to tell various stories of what I had missed whilst I had been out all night. I soon became rigid and explained very apologetically that I needed to leave. With the help of others, I removed myself from the club, knowing they would be carrying me home if I remained any longer. However, I did make sure that the home-made apple crumble that Elaine created for me joined me for the journey home. Once home, with apple crumble in hand, I crawled up the stairs one step at a time and pushed the bowl of perfection along the floor as I went. I made it to the bedside cabinet where I placed my indulgence. There, it would wait for me, whilst I manoeuvred myself to the en-suite, into the shower for a hose down, and back onto the bed without leaving my crawling position. Lying, still naked, and slightly propped by pillows, I proceeded to shovel the crumble down like a man possessed, falling asleep halfway through the bowl. I know I was halfway through because I woke 30 minutes later, still with the bowl in one hand, spoon in the other, and apple sauce dribbling down my chin and onto my chest. Finishing off the treat, I returned to dreamland, waking up a couple of hours later with the most agonising pain in my legs. Someone had driven over my legs whilst I was asleep, I was sure of it. They didn't belong to me anymore, and they didn't obey any command. The rest of the day was spent intermittently, either in a comatose state or dragging myself by my elbows to the toilet, or downstairs for dinner, which I still couldn't eat. Never having felt 100 miles of tarmac abuse on the skeleton before, this was a different and new kind of pain. It was 3am when I awoke up, needing another visit to the throne for a pee. With one eye open, I decided to try the vertical position, and tentatively shifting my weight onto my feet, I stood up. I could stand! Euphorically, I tried the walk. I could walk too, even if I did look like Bambi on ice. I made it to the toilet on my feet, but with a huge amount of blister pain. That was ok, though. I knew blister pain - I was happy with blister pain - I have needed to cope with it so many times in the past, it almost felt homely. I smiled from ear to ear and went back to sleep. As the alarm sounded at 5.30, I fell into some clothes, staggered down the stairs, drank a couple of cups of coffee and headed out the door for a 13-hour shift, seven hours of which were to be coaching, and then an interview with the local BBC news channel.

As I slowly descended the driveway at 6.30am, peering through the slightly murky screen with glazed eyes, a ghostly jogger silently sailed over the end of the road. As my gaze ventured further on past the early-risen athlete, I admired the low-level mist smothering the greenery of the country park, only allowing the pinnacles of the tallest vegetation to feel the full effect of a new dawn; a new beginning, a new chapter. This is exactly how I felt as I continued to the end of the road and turned right. Those few seconds, as I encapsulated the entirety of the gliding jogger as he passed through the autumnal picture in front of me, stopped time and left a very deep lasting impression. I knew then that everything was going to be different. If I continued this journey with the same drive, self-knowing, hard work and enthusiasm, continuing to learn from past and present failures or successes, then I would be able to answer some of those questions... what is possible? What is my limit? What is my maximum effort?

Continuing along the tarmac, I couldn't help looking over at the runner with an overwhelming warmth that came from a place of pride, knowing I had trodden that path time and time again, while going through a spectrum of emotions and pain to finish the first hurdle, and becoming ultimately aware that my failures, once acknowledged, were my biggest weapons. I could also feel every step he was taking, every breath he was inhaling, and every change in wind direction. I even whispered to him, "Be careful", as he passed over an invisible but slight undulation in the asphalt. He, of course, misplaced his step, immediately recovering. I knew it was there, just like every other crack, curb, pothole, smell, incline and invasive shrub that continued to grow, dominating the path next to it. This was now my route and it belonged to me. I'd laid down the foundations for others to use it. I actually felt I had become a part of Lutterworth, my senses fully aware of everything the town had to offer throughout a whole 24-hour period. This might sound overdramatic, but I had spent possibly 30 out of my 47 years walking, running and playing on these streets, but never really knowing them. I was suddenly aware of Lutterworth and its energy. In many ways, I will look back on this event as my biggest success. It has paved the way and laid a foundation for everything else in front of me to benefit from.

Recovery progressed at a staggering pace. Within 48 hours I was able to cover a slow 3-miles on the treadmill, and a nine mile walk the day after. By the end of the week, I was back to full training, and building for the virtual London Marathon I was going to run with Sylvia the following weekend. No blood, no illness, no convulsions; just very hungry and a couple of friendly blisters on the feet. Job done, lessons learnt, progress made, and a massive confidence boost. Don't get me wrong, mistakes were still made, but every experience is a chance to learn. I believe my nutrition and hydration weren't in the right place, and I also ran in the wrong shoes, too hard for tarmac. If there's grass next to the path, use it. Every soft footstep helps. The objective of the event was to cover 100 miles, not to necessarily race it, so I planned the chart below to show expected finish times of each lap. This helped more than I thought it would by having the ability to see, in small increments, if I was too slow or too fast. I continue to use this visual help from that day with every event.

One last thing; the successful finish on the Grim Reaper was finished in 25 hours and 56 minutes; four minutes before the cut off time. 100 miles around Lutterworth was completed in 22 hours 53 minutes, over three hours faster.

Lap 1	4.5 m	10.52am	10.40am	-2mins
Lap 2	9.1m	11.26am	11.20pm	-6mins
Lap 3	13.6m	12.12pm	12.00pm	-12mins
Lap 4	18.2m	1.00pm	12.54pm	-6mins
Lap 5	22.7m	1.50pm	1.45pm	-5mins

Lap 6	27.3m	2.42pm	2.42pm	0
Lap 7	31.8m	3.36pm	3.52pm	+6mins
Lap 8	36.4m	4.32pm	4.40pm	+8mins
Lap 9	40.9m	5.30pm	5.38pm	+8mins
Lap 10	45.5m	6.30pm	6.34pm	+4mins
Lap 11	50.0m	7.32pm	7.32pm	+3mins
Lap 12	54.6m	8.36pm	8.40pm	+4mins
Lap 13	59.1m	9.42pm	9.45pm	+3mins
Lap 14	63.7m	10.50pm	10.50pm	0
Lap 15	68.2m	0.00am	0.00am	0
Lap 16	72.8m	1.12am	1.11am	-1mins
Lap 17	77.3m	2.26am	1.22am	-4mins
Lap 18	81.9m	3.42am	3.48am	+6mins
Lap 19	86.4m	5.00am	5.05am	+5mins
Lap 20	91.0m	6.20am	6.19am	-1min
Lap 21	95.5m	7.42am	7.31am	-11mins
Lap 22	100m	9.06am	8.53am	-13mins

Chapter 13
Training (Part 2)

September (Part 2)

My enthusiasm and my drive all but disappeared after the 100 miles around Lutterworth. It seemed to blanket my fire; I needed a way to ignite the flames again. Going out for a five-mile jog or walk once again became hard. I couldn't get up early and I was struggling in the dark again. I second questioned myself over every decision, and I started believing the email from Martin could have had a deeper impact than I first gave it credit for. I was looking for answers in anything. Could I just be over training? Was I in control of my basics? I always refer to my basics when I'm struggling mentally, or physically. My five basic rules are something I call on when I'm not right. I ask myself these questions first, before moving onto anything else: Am I eating nutritionally? Am I keeping hydrated? Am I sleeping enough? Am I exercising daily? And - am I breathing fresh air for an hour or two each day? Whatever the issue, one of these has usually slipped, but this time they all seemed to be in order.

Staring at the wallpaper one morning, I realised this slow drop in enthusiasm started a week or so before the equinox; maybe it was just the psychological connection to a cool down that is expected as part of any training program when building up to a challenge. I had reduced my mileage and training, and I was sleeping more. I had never really trained specifically for an event before, as you well know, so had never felt the concluding part of a training program. The body is a remarkable machine and reacts instantly to any change, either positively or negatively. Any increased change in movement or strength related work needed from the body, will have a mirrored reaction in energy levels or strength capabilities, either improving performance, speed or endurance, just as it would if a reduction in energy expectation was felt, thereby producing lower energy and performance levels. Any change in strength requirement will have a mirrored reaction in muscle hypertrophy (increase in size or strength), or muscle atrophy (decrease in size or strength). Equally, any change in sleep patterns, diet, hydration or stress will force a change in the direction that is required to cope with the lifestyle adjustment.

It's worth remembering that your mind is only as old as you are, i.e., your calendar years. This could be 10, 26, 57 or even 90 years old, and makes microsecond by microsecond decisions based on your personal history and experiences. Most of the time, these decisions are what your subconscious believes to be better for you in respect of what will make you the happiest, most relaxed or the most comfortable. Your hormones, however, have a vast amount of knowledge stretching back millions of years, making instantaneous decisions on unaccountable scenarios, encounters, dangers, pleasures and discussions. These decisions are purely made to increase our chances of survival, in order to pass on our gene pool and allow us to evolve. Just looking at the past two and a half million years, when we first came out of the trees, our hormones have been learning how to help us survive second by second. We lived a remarkably similar lifestyle for 99% of these two and a half million years; living in caves, hunting and gathering, fighting for food and keeping ourselves and our family alive. This is where your hormones still live.

This is how and why we needed to build or reduce muscle mass. Muscle fibres require energy to exist; the more muscle mass you hold, the more calories you burn. Why waste unnecessary energy on maintaining muscle fibres if we don't need them to live the lifestyle, we currently live. You've heard the term 'us it or lose it'. If it's not needed, your hormones will reduce skeletal muscle to reduce daily calorie expenditure; obviously not good if you are trying to lose body fat. Your hormones believe they are doing you a favour by doing this. Food was scarce for majority of our ancestral history. We would need to save every calorie we could before the harsh winter hit, and a massive reduction in the availability of food would be experienced. Carrying a few extra kilograms of fat in autumn could be our saviour if we had to battle through a hard, long winter, so fat was more important to our survival than excess muscle. Now, though, we live in nice warm houses with wardrobes full of fashionable clothing, capable of keeping us snug in all weathers. Unfortunately, we still put on the kilograms but don't experience the harsh winters as we once did, so obesity has grown to one in three people.

This instantaneous hormonal reaction to your environment is also the reason why you receive more energy. When you ask for more, more will be provided. You won't receive the extra energy needed to go to the gym a couple of hours a week until you've been to the gym for a couple of hours a week and asked for it. Look at it this way. As far as your stress hormones 'cortisol' and 'adrenaline' are concerned, the lovely, safe, early morning jog around the local park isn't a lovely, safe, early morning jog. It is a jog for survival; It could mean you are tracking a possible meal, or it could mean you are concerned for safety and feel the need to escape a predator. In either case, if you return home sweaty and out of breath, hormonally, you are at your limits. If this is the case, their reaction to this would be to make a slight change to your physical capabilities and increase your energy levels for tomorrow, just in case a similar situation presents itself. This would result in a more comfortable outcome and an increased chance of survival. Therefore, our lungs increase in their gaseous exchange capabilities and perform optimally when pushed a few times a week and in turn persuade the heart to become a little stronger to cope with the higher demand for oxygen if we need to run faster to survive. Mr Arnold Schwarzenegger grew a massive physique, not because he lifted iron every day; it was because his hormones believed he was wrestling a wild hog, fighting a sabre-toothed tiger or chopping wood for heat and food, every day. He took himself to his limits every day, so the hormonal reaction to this was to supply more muscle mass for him to have a better chance of survival, should he need to fight again tomorrow - which he did - every day for 30 plus years. If the fighting was to stop, the muscle would atrophy. Like I said, why keep excess calorie-burning muscle fibres if the environment and lifestyle don't require it. It's a waste of resources.

My lethargy grew because I was slowing down in preparation for the 100 miles. I wasn't asking for as much energy; therefore, I wasn't given as much energy. My lifestyle had become less drastic and less dependent on the resilience needed day by day for survival. After only a couple of weeks of this, I physically and mentally started to relax, resulting in the relevant hormones to respond as evolution taught them too.

Post event, I found it equally as difficult to find the enthusiasm to continue training; this is natural. Once again, it's the fault of the hormones.

For a couple of weeks after an event as challenging as this was, some hormone concentrations change within the blood. Adrenaline levels drop, with cortisol and prolactin levels increasing. Adrenaline makes the heart beat faster.

In turn, this increases blood flow to the brain and muscles, and encourages the development of more sugar to be used for fuel. So, a reduction of adrenaline would do the opposite, decreasing blood sugars and flow to the brain, bringing on diminished mental resolve and an increasing level of depression. This is why people suffer from a condition called 'Post Event Blues', after a race. Enhanced cortisol levels instigate anxiety, and as the system feels it's in a consistent state of low-level stress, it brings on a permanent feeling of fight or flight. Prolactin is a hormone that both men and women have, but it can increase 10 to 20 times the normal amount when a woman is pregnant. This helps the development of milk and is a contributor to the emotional rollercoaster they feel during and after pregnancy. Prolactin also increases dramatically post-event. Therefore, I developed a new ability to randomly cry at inconsequential adverts on the TV. Add these three hormone irregularities together and you have an emotional cocktail capable of irrational behaviour, irregular sleep patterns, bad food cravings, and mood swings a teenager would be proud of.

All said and done, September was a game of two halves, each as challenging as the other.

October

Strangely, supporting Sylvia on the 4th of October, whilst she fought her way through the Virtual London Marathon, was how I re-established my greed for more. I was back - or so I thought!

The darker nights and cooler weather very quickly made their presence known. For the first time I was able to connect with the race. Greeting some days at 4am with blurred-junky eyes, stiff joints, achy muscles and a preliminary thought of, "Please no, not another day" bouncing around my head as my phone vibrated on the bedside cabinet. This suddenly became real. If I want to win this race, I had to remind myself daily, that I must win it before the gun echoes on the start line. Our club mantra is infused in the deepest darkest part of my temporal lobe; deep within my hippocampus... 'ONE BREATH, ONE STEP, ONE SECOND AT A TIME'... I repeated this mantra in my head most mornings as I awoke at silly o'clock. I would start to count...one, two, and as I said three, I reluctantly sat up; then another count, one, two, and three as I would force myself to my feet. By the time I repeated this process ten times, I would be sitting at the dining table with a black coffee in one hand and a pint of water in the other. The day would now look less daunting as I started to plan the day's activities. How many of this month's 350-mile target will I have time for, after I've considered work, family time, stretching, Wim Hof's breathing method, a cold shower, a couple of thousand words in the book, and food preparation. Life had switched, I was now going to work for a rest!

Days were starting to blend into each other. I would find myself looking back to September and wishing I was there. I spent every day in October chasing the miles. With one week of the month to go, I was nearly 30 miles behind and beginning to feel I had bitten off more than I could chew. Negative thoughts entwined their way through every decision. My food choices weren't the best, I started relying on caffeine to get me through the day, and my separation anxiety had crept back in. This type of anxiety first began when I was a truck driver with ASDA, and Teri was at the peak of her disability. Most days I would speak to my wife whilst driving around the country with a deep thirst to be home, where I would be able to help and support her. After a few years of this, the anxiety became volcanic, driving me to tears of panic as I drove the truck further and further away from our hometown every day. I hadn't felt this for a couple of years, until now. With the lack of sleep, poor food choices, dehydration and longer nights, this anxiety even turned into agoraphobia on some mornings. I would spend 30 to 40 minutes walking towards and away from the front door, before I managed to escape and reach the first corner of the street. Some days I would accumulate between 12 and 15 miles by continually walking around the block because I couldn't force myself to venture further afield.

October was a battle through every one of the 31 days, and this resulted in me experiencing my first illness in over 8 years. I developed a bloody cold, and in the same fashion as I would treat anyone else in my world when they had a similar illness, I took it as a sign that I wasn't doing it right. I accepted the warning and decided to step up and stop feeling sorry for myself. I promised myself that November would be different. I had to get back on track. I couldn't afford to fail another month. I had not only finished the month five miles short, but I had failed the month's challenge which was to accomplish, on two separate occasions, a 32-mile day consisting of two four-hour walks with a 20-minute break between for food. This was how I was going to tackle the event, and I had to start including this in my training. Four months to go and it was only going to get harder.

November

As November started, my illness subsided. I felt fresh, eager and ready to fight. Training started becoming part of life again, and as much as I still had to rely on the counting of one, two, three, and the club mantra on repeat every morning, there wasn't as much resistance. The reality of the event was itching away under my skin. I could feel it some days like a bucket of cold water washing over me. There was no plan B; a successful outcome was the only option; there were too many people watching. Hundreds of people around the town were starting to become inquisitive. Newspapers and local news channels were keeping an eye on me, and this book was reliant on a successful conclusion. If my goal was to create awareness of my challenge and introduce extra pressure to succeed, then I'd scored.

November 5th, and a second lockdown hit the UK. Covid-19 was rapidly increasing again, and the decision was made to shut all non-essential businesses unless you could work from home. Reluctantly, this meant that I had to lock the doors of the club once again. Still not financially recovered from the first lockdown, times could very quickly become difficult if the lockdown was to last past Christmas. I had no choice in this matter, so quickly moved my energy to things that were in my control. I used this as a gift to concentrate on training and writing. By halfway through the month, I had already put 200 miles on the legs and spent hours in front of the laptop. I felt in control, moving forward more positively than I had for weeks.

With 375 miles in the training programme, I only had two issues; the endless miles on my own would develop a loneliness, and this loneliness was fast becoming part of the day. When people came into my day, I sometimes struggled with the skill to chit chat. I also felt constantly hungry; I just couldn't satisfy my need to eat. I was sure I was swallowing 4000 calories a day just to keep up with the energy demands. Christmas was poking its head around the corner and family time took priority, meaning I only managed a couple of big mileage days, hitting a strong 40 miler halfway through the month. Overall, I was incredibly happy with progress, and I was loving the challenge of the wintry weather. Keeping to the plan, I was still maintaining plenty of bodyweight training and a couple of circuit classes each week.

December
December was when it really hit me. As soon as the first of the month was crossed off the calendar, my attitude

changed. The club was able to open again and required my attention. Miles became easy again; 400 miles was the target. Getting out of bed at three or four in the morning on my days off work didn't even require the mantra or the counting; writing this book became so fluid, and my focus once again shifted to the precision needed to be successful in every aspect of this challenge to make it all come together. I started thinking about the positioning of items in the sled for perfect balance; food choices, and how I would manage to eat 5000 calories a day whilst still moving. Hydration choices needed my attention, with regard to how many electrolytes and how many hot or cold drinks I would need; my route choices, after taking into account obstructions like high curbs and narrow paths or no paths - I didn't want to be a hazard to anyone. Where could I sleep safely; there was still the chance an opportunist could take advantage of hundreds of pounds worth of food and clothing that were sitting in my sled whilst I was asleep in the tent; and what time of the day I would start and finish, as I still wanted to maintain a reasonably normal sleep pattern, even if it was for only three to four hours a night. The sled started to make regular appearances, with the comfort of it increasing. The sled was starting to feel part of the journey, but I still felt somewhat embarrassed whilst walking through town, so continually asked friends and family to join me.

After I woke up in the middle of the night on the 21st in a massive panic, the tempo of the training increased once again. I had spent the whole night thinking I wasn't doing enough, not enough mileage and not enough long days. I hadn't sampled the food I was going to eat enough; I hadn't used my small portable stove yet and I hadn't ordered spare parts for the sled. I hadn't even practised the official route to see how long it was, or how long it would take or if the sled would cope with the ups and downs. However, I had done a couple of 40 milers but hadn't experienced the required distance needed on the event each day, which was 60 miles, and hadn't even been over 10 miles with the sled. This morning was also significant because it meant I had less than 10-weeks to go until the 1st of March, which was probably where the panic attack came from. It did give me another kick up the arse, though. By the end of the month, I had planned the route and practised it numerous times, with and without the sled. The 400 miles for the month was smashed as I finished on 410 miles. Samples of the race food had been ordered and used, and sleeping locations arranged, which was to be the club, a tent in my back garden and my van. The van would be parked at the industrial estate security office car park, halfway around the route, and the sled was now starting to fill up with race equipment and feeling a part of me. By the end of the year, I was in control, but nervousness was growing. The only way I could control my nerves was to be constructive.

January
It's the last month of big miles, with the target of 425 miles smashed out the park. I had one job to do on the weekends, and that simply was to cover miles - as many as possible. Weekdays were full of jogging, bodyweight exercises, circuit classes, and on Wednesdays, an extra-long 10-hour training day with some of the day spent with the sled, making the event food with the stove, and covering the expected route. During the long days, I would imagine every possibility that could hinder my progress, or even finish my race, and I would build strategies of how to remedy those problems. These were then added to my toolbox.

Another lockdown was introduced near the beginning of the month, but I didn't even think about it. It just allowed me to be single-minded and to further fall into the preparations.

This is it – eight weeks of solid training. Every aspect of the race was being pulled together. Mile after mile, playing with the sled, eating the right foods, keeping hydrated, randomly waking up to start the day at awkward times and, on two occasions, leaving the house at one minute past midnight to walk until midday, as this would be the start time of the event on the 1st of March. On one of these occasions, Mikey joined me from two until six in the morning as we walked the streets of Lutterworth without another soul in sight. I have always loved the kind of conversation that seems to arise when it's 3am. This reminded me of a party at the turn of the millennium when I was in Scotland with my family. We were in the middle of a three-day drinking frenzy. It was around 3am, and I was sat on the floor in a cousin's kitchen with my brother-in-law at the time for two hours, deep in conversation about who was the best vocalist; Freddie Mercury or George Michael. The debate was immense, well-structured and sincere; well, that's what it sounded like from the inside, but if you were a fly on the wall, listening in, I would imagine it came across like a pair of drunken bums trying to construct sentences. The outcome of the two-hour conversation was that George Michael was the best vocalist, but Freddie Mercury was the best entertainer. Anyway, the conversation with Mikey, during those four hours walking down the middle of abandoned roads in Lutterworth, was just as informative and life changing. If the politicians, world leaders, CEOs of globally influential companies could have heard our points of view, it could have solved every one of the issues our planet is facing today. We were economists, politicians, scientists, influencers, and innovators - even if it was just for those few hours!

I was gifted with the perfect weather for the last weekend of the month. A nice dump of snow fell within a few hours on Sunday morning, and I enjoyed every single second of it, marking the end of a perfect training month. 520 miles accumulated - 95 more than was set on the table. A few aches and pains, but nothing more than would be expected by anyone who was averaging nearly seventeen miles every day for a whole month.

February

Here it is - the last four weeks. Cool down time, and I was ready for it. Legs were tired, my whole body was tight, eyes bloodshot, and nerves a little edgy. Daily miles progressively slowed down, allowing time for more technical training. I did feel ready, though, I was nervous, excited, apprehensive, but ready. I had done everything I had set out to do and, if anything, a little more. I couldn't believe it. I did the training and it felt good. The confidence that came from knowing I had done the miles, maintained physical strength, stretched, practised using the equipment, ate the foods, overcame scenarios time after time and held off injury, was more powerful than I thought it was going to be.

Why hadn't I done this before? Why did it take eight years of messing about to discover this energy boost? I can now tell you - it's a much friendlier way to approach a challenge, and a much comfier cushion to place your head on the night before.

February is always a quick month, but the first 25 days just vanished. I went to bed on the first and woke up 350 miles later, with only 72 hours left, before last orders were to be announced. Such a strange 72 hours. Every minute was felt. If I were asleep, I was dreaming about it; if I were eating, I was thinking I was fuelling the engine; if I were watching a film, only half the brain would be paying attention to the storyline whilst the other half was going over scenarios; if I were showering, I was making sure I made a note of how enjoyable it felt, so I could call back on it, when needed, to encourage me to get to the end. All I did for those last few days was eat, sleep, stretch and dream, until it was time to leave the nest... GULP!

Chapter 14
Let the Games Begin

It was four in the afternoon, eight hours before I was to leave our club to take the first step of what would turn out to be over 800,000 steps to complete the job. I had been slowly changing my body clock over the week leading to the big day so that the 3am starts would feel more comfortable. The alarm was set for 10pm, which meant I had a potential six hours of sleep available to me; but as you can probably guess, the reality turned out to be more like two, spending the other four hours tossing and turning, shivering and sweating. It felt like an eternity before the anticipated double buzz vibrated my phone on the set of drawers from across the room, telling me it was time. There was no more count down, no more contemplation. I was about to feel everything I had been visualising over the past few months.

Ninety minutes later I was fed, watered, dressed and in the passenger seat of my van, being driven to the club. I was too nervous to drive myself, so Teri did the honours, although she seemed as nervous as I did. Pulling up outside the club, the industrial estate had a lonely, still, even eerie feel to it. Teri and I silently unloaded the last of my belongings out of the van and into the club, along with all my food for the week. The food had been separated into seven separate bags, one for each day. This way I could closely monitor how many calories I was consuming each day. Each bag consisted of three freeze-dried expedition meal packs, three packets of porridge oats, two protein cookies, six Nutella pancakes, one thousand calories of trail mix, two bags of beef jerky, four Babybel cheeses and three nutrient bars; all adding up to approximately 6000 calories. I knew my calorie expenditure was going to be between of 8000 and 9000, but I felt that trying to consume 6000 would be hard enough.

It wasn't long before a small crowd gathered in and around the club, including Steve, Sylvia's son. He was in the process of making a documentary about me and the challenge. Steve, who's a bit of a rocker, is a drummer in a band called Vambo, but his artistic talents don't stop with the drums. He has a flare for anything arty, like drawing, painting, and writing. We were also about to discover that photography, producing and editing would become part of his ever-increasing skill set. He had a drone hovering somewhere above us, three separate cameras artistically arranged around the start line, and another pointing directly into my face as he conducted one last pre-race interview with me. Four attempts it took him to record an adequate interview as I repeatedly mumbled, lost the plot, and generally cocked it up through nerves, each time becoming more frustrated with myself and the chores I had to do because I was finding it harder to concentrate, as the clock was ticking closer to one minute past midnight.

I was accompanied on this virtual challenge by forty other athletes from around the world, all of them taking on the 380 mile 6633 Arctic Ultra. In addition to this, a further 100 athletes took on the shorter 120-mile version of the race. This is also a version of the race available in Canada. The 120 race finishes at Fort MacPherson, the third checkpoint of the 380 race. Eight of the participants for the shorter race were also members of the club, including my wife and Sylvia. They were both keen to join me when I left the club, firstly to keep me company, and secondly to start registering their own miles for the race.

Unsure and overwhelmed by the task in front of me, I stood in front of all my supporters as they waited patiently for the expected speech. They expected a minute or two of profound words of wisdom from me to lift them and inspire them before I would disappear into the bleakness of the night, but I was speechless. Eventually, I managed a few vowels or grunts, but nothing with any substance; just a few words squeezed out of the appreciation I felt towards them for turning up at midnight on this cold, still, daunting Sunday evening. Then, just as I was about to get into full flow and open my heart to them, someone mentioned I had 90 seconds to go.

My heart rate instantly increased as I leapt out of the club doors to strap myself onto the front of the sled. With cameras flashing from all directions and the buzz of the drone circling my head I felt dizzy with anticipation, my bowels rumbled and rolled as they tried to inform me of a possible movement. Sweat started to roll down my back, whilst at the same time I began shivering as the mercury bottomed out at minus one degree Celsius. I needed to start; I needed to release the nerves before they overshadowed the task at hand, and I would find a way to escape. "Come on..." I murmured to myself, "How long to go?" I raised my voice to the crowd. "30 seconds" came a reply. How had all the getting ready only taken 60 seconds? Time had frozen. "Come on..." I once again murmured a little louder; I need to go now, as I shook like a child in the waiting room of a dentist. "GO!" came a voice from the crowd, and I was off through a barrage of clapping and cheering, away from the club, through the gates and up the road with the sled in tow, and with Teri and Sylvia keeping me company for the first few miles. There was a journey ahead hidden in the dark miles down the road that would inevitably change me.

Day 1, 75 miles
Teri accompanied me for the first five miles, but then headed home as she had an early rise and a busy day

ahead of her. Sylvia continued for a further five before retreating to her bed for the night. She really didn't want to leave me but had planned to re-join the escapade later in the afternoon. She also knew Mikey was to join me within the hour and walk into the daylight with me. Mikey and I had developed a nice habit of walking into the daytime over the past few months. It's a special time of the day, witnessing the world come to life: the birds start singing at the slightest glimmer of light, the frost grows on the grass as the temperature drops around 5am, and then the mist begins to blanket the shrubbery in the fields at around 7am when the temperature starts to rise again as the sun winks at us from a place where the earth meets the sky. I noticed the ever-increasing frequency of interruptions and disturbances from the night's silence as the symphony of life's noises come from traffic, car horns, dogs barking, cats fighting, and the reverse warning beeps of delivery trucks bringing goods to fill up the shelves of the local coffee house, baker's and butchers. All this reminded me that life is continuing regardless of my adventure, most of them totally oblivious of the world I am currently residing in.

Mikey's appearance in the distance at 3.30am was a comfort. I had only been on my own for an hour but felt rather self-conscious and a little concerned about walking the streets with a sled full of valuables on my own; this feeling, as the week continued, became less of an issue though.

Some of the strangest sights are seen in the early hours. The first one we came across was a group of late teenagers or early 20-year-olds walking, giggling and softly singing as they were obviously returning from a joyful night out somewhere, regardless of the lockdown rules – but, hey-ho. This was on the opposite side of the road to us, and what made it entertaining was one of them was comfortably sat in a shopping trolley and being pushed by the others. Further along the same road a few minutes later we came across a young man dressed in jeans, a white t-shirt, and wrapped in a silver emergency blanket to keep warm; he was also walking in the opposite direction. Now, before I go any further, you need to understand that Lutterworth is a quiet market town, so witnessing a person in a shopping trolley being pushed by their drunken mates was unusual, but adding to that, seeing a solitude person walking along the streets wrapped in a silver blanket, as if he had just survived some sort of disaster was as rare as an alien landing site. We approached him to see if he was okay and if we could help. He promptly replied with, "Is this the way to Coventry?" A little shocked, and after one of those glances between myself and Mikey that can mean a thousand words, we replied, "You're around 25 miles away and heading in the wrong direction". To which he tried to explain his predicament of being robbed and left in Lutterworth by the police to find his way home. He had no money, no phone and no idea where he was, but was insistent that he was okay and incredibly grateful for our help in pointing him in the right direction. Then he continued to walk away in the correct direction. We happened to be going in the same direction for the next few minutes so followed on the opposite side of the road. Feeling we needed to do a little more to help, we approached him before our paths separated and gave him some warm clothes as it was below zero degrees. To this day we have never heard what happened to him, or my hoodie with the club's logo on the front: did he make it to Coventry? One last thing that always makes us chuckle when reminiscing of the incident, and one of the strange things about the encounter, was that he never once acknowledged or questioned why I was pulling a five-foot sled on wheels, with a bag tied to it that resembled the shape of a human body, and in the middle of the night...is that a normal sight in Coventry - ha-ha?

Progressing well, and with nearly 40 miles into the day, I received a phone call from Leicester Radio asking if they could do a live interview with me to talk about my challenge and the charity for which I am raising funding. "Of course," I replied. "Great, just hold the line for a couple of minutes and you'll be introduced into the conversation live on the radio, so don't swear". Ha-ha, what's the first thing you want to do when someone tells you not to do something? Do that exact thing, ha-ha. I spent the next seven minutes continually repeating to myself not to swear. I didn't know what I was saying because of the fear of blurting out a forbidden word. This interview continued to entertain me for a couple of hours afterwards as I chuckled to myself thinking about the repercussions that could have accompanied some foul language. Years before, I remembered someone saying there is no such thing as bad publicity. This made me think, that, maybe I should have slipped up and let out a soft naughty word or two; it could have been the perfect way to grab some attention.

Just after lunchtime, Sylvia re-joined me for the afternoon. The legs were becoming tired, and I could feel a couple of blisters forming, so enjoyed some company. Most of our discussion that afternoon was reminiscing about how our journeys had ended up here, walking endlessly around Lutterworth, on a virtual Arctic race while dragging a sled. The next few hours passed quickly as we were lost in our little world, and it wasn't long before Teri met me for the last couple of hours of the day. I still feel extremely gifted when I look back at how the relationship between Teri and me has changed. From starting with having to look after a disabled wife, to progressing amazingly to having a wife who now offers me more strength than anyone else in my life, and is

189

physically capable of more than the average 50-year-old. This is why I always preferred to leave Teri's company until the end of the day, when I'm struggling the most. She is always the one that can get me to achieve more.

It was eight in the evening when I gave up for the day and arrived at the club for some food and sleep; but before the nice stuff, attention had to be given to my ailments. Feet went into an ice-bucket and I spent 20 minutes stretching. I prepared the sled for the next day, filled water containers, organised food for easy access, and arranged clothing for quick assembly. Settling into the sleeping bag at quarter to nine and with the alarm set for two in the morning, it still took over two hours to fall asleep. The throbbing in my legs and feet, along with the anticipation of the next day, drove me nuts as I shuffled from one side to the other. I was just about to say, "Sod it, I may as well get up and start walking", when my phone alarm echoed around the club.

Day 2, 48 miles

Rushing out the door to meet Mikey at 3am, my poor legs didn't feel too bad. I was pleasantly surprised, considering I had done 75 miles in 20 hours pulling a sled after only having a couple of hours sleep. Excellent, I thought, time for another long, relentless day. It wasn't long, though, before I became annoyed with the sled. Something felt different; it felt heavier, and we must have stopped four or five times to adjust the layout of the items to create a more comfortable balance. The sled only had one axle, making it pivot in the middle, and the position of the supplies was vital so there wasn't too much weight on my shoulders, but enough to prevent it bouncing as I moved. The previous 75-mile day seemed perfect, but today, even though everything was in the same place, it felt heavy. Mikey insisted it was just because I was tired from the slog the previous day. We marched on for a couple of hours with our usual chit chat, talking about what's wrong with the world and how we would put it to rights. Once the birds started chirping and singing, the discussion changed, as it always does, to what's right with the world. The sled, however, didn't change, and continued to feel heavy.

Later in the afternoon, Sylvia joined me once again. I was starting to hit the first of many dark holes. I wasn't in the mood to talk, so we both listened to our own music and walked next to each other for a few hours. I was noticeably losing time on every mile, and my feet were barely making it off the ground. I grabbed my walking poles for support with the hope I could pick up the pace, but each mile took longer and longer, the poles did help as I leant on them to keep me vertical. It was only five in the afternoon when I signalled to Sylvia I was heading back to base. We both removed our earphones to hear squeaks coming from the sled. Both wheels were intermittently turning and squeaking. For a second they would turn, and then, for the next second, they would resist the forward motion and force me to drag them. This, of course, had worn down the tyres to the point where I could nearly see thread through the rubber. This, I now understood, was why the sled had felt heavy all day; this is why the sled no longer pushed me down the hills and this is why I now had a bad back, bad hips, jelly-like legs, and feet that were in for more of a mess than the day before. Pissed off, I stormed into the club around 5.30pm and called it a day, only covering 48 miles.

What was I to do? Sitting with a big mug of hot chocolate and my feet in the ice-bucket, I went over my options. It was impossible to take the sled out for another day. I couldn't get spares for the sled as I had tried before the event, but it was an old set-up and hard to find spares. The rules of the race, however, didn't state that I had to pull a sled or even carry anything. In fact, I was only one of maybe four or five racers that wanted to make the race feel as authentic as possible by using a sled. However, I did still feel I needed to know if I could cover the distance whilst being ladened down. So, the only option was to carry what I could in my trusted rucksack. Filling it each day with my clothes, medical bag, and food and water for the day, it wasn't too heavy - around 30 pounds (15 kilograms) - but it was heavy enough to give me a little taste of what I wanted.

Alarm set once again for 2am, I was in bed before 8pm. Now, with throbbing legs, burning feet, a stiff back and angry hips, sleep was impossible, but I refused stubbornly to give up, maybe grabbing a couple more hours.

Day 3, 54 miles

The night was long and frustrating before the alarm demanded I rose from my cocoon. Mikey was to meet me at 3am for the third morning in succession, and this was the first time that having this appointment with him was the biggest incentive that made me get up and out. Still in a lot of pain in my back and hips, from dragging a disabled sled the day before, I wobbled and winced my way towards the outskirts of Lutterworth to meet my nocturnal partner. He could see I was in a mess, so after the usual morning greetings, we walked in silence as he realised, I wasn't in a chatty mood.

I'm not sure if it was intentional, but our rhythm began mirroring each other's; our feet hit the ground in unison and our arms swung to the same beat. Eventually, my breathing imitated his, my posture changed, my speed increased, and my vision became tunnelled. After a few miles, Mikey softly started talking to me about breath, how powerful it can be, and the acceptance of it; allowing the outside world to become part of you, filling up every cell with pure, clean, life-giving oxygen, then exhaling all the impurities on the out breath. I learnt to focus my mind on the rhythm of breathing in and breathing out, controlling it, feeling it, using it; releasing all other thoughts and just concentrating on the purity of breathing. Then, with that, the world went silent again. The only sound I could hear was the roll of the rubber on the sole of my trainers as they glided over the footpath; the steady flow of air inflating and deflating my lungs, and occasionally, my heartbeat whenever I was able to drop even deeper. We stayed in this meditative state for a couple of hours. All pain subsided, time passed unnoticed, and we seemed to move as one. It wasn't until the day started to break and the birds started chirping that we snapped out of it, realising we had covered 10 miles and it was time for our traditional morning coffee.

Mikey is an amazing teacher; like me, he lives how he educates others. He lives his life looking for contentment and acceptance, teaching Tai-Chi and meditation, absorbing book after book about spirituality, the foundations of religions, belief structures, creativity and energies. He instinctively knew what I needed that morning, and without a word, pulled me in. I continued to use it through the challenge and, to this day, when I'm feeling the stresses of life.

On this day, when I needed it the most, friendship came through. Jonny visited me for a few miles, with a coffee and an uplifting chat about how we were going to tackle the Arctic next year. Then Mikey drove past and handed me a home-made large cob, filled with bacon, once again reading my mind. After I had demolished that, Karen, my old Sunday running buddy, came into view and enticed me to walk past her home where she came running out with some home-made warm banana bread smothered with butter. By noon, the day was starting to feel better, and a smile found its place on my face as I started dancing to the music in my ears. I trod mile after mile in my own world before Sylvia turned up. We happily chatted for a few miles before she handed me over to Teri for the last four-mile loop of Lutterworth. But Teri, I'm afraid, didn't get the best of me that day. I was again broken, and she was my rock who lovingly, but sternly, encouraged me to the completion of day three.

Staggering through the door of my house - I know that, as part of my challenge, I wasn't supposed to set foot in my home, but my feet needed medical attention. I crawled upstairs with Teri following so she could address my ailments. I removed my shoes and socks to witness the two feet-shaped lumps. They were swollen beyond recognition. The blisters had blended into each other, and they were purple. Minutes later I screamed in pain as a sensation rolled over my feet like a steam roller. The girls came running in from their rooms, panicking because they thought something had happened. This unrelenting agony lasted for two and a half hours, forcing me to scream, cry and moan so much it nearly made my daughters cry. I could see in their eyes they were feeling my pain. The only reprieve came when Teri squeezed all my toes in her two hands as tight as she could, which of course angered the blisters, but the pain felt from squashing blisters was nothing compared to the initial pain.

There had to be an easier way of doing this I said. Moving for 18 hours a day was destroying me. I couldn't do another day like this. I must admit, if I were currently in the Arctic, instead of hiking around Lutterworth, the pain I was feeling that evening would have pulled me out of the event. I would undoubtedly have quit. I needed to change my approach. I desperately needed a new plan.

Day 4, 55 miles

Passing out in my own bed as the pain eased just before midnight, I woke up a couple of hours later and shuffled down the stairs, one step at a time, on my bum. My feet were still feeling the effects of the night before as they throbbed, almost visually, like a scene from a Tom and Jerry cartoon, where Tom had been smashed on the foot with a hammer. Each morning my feet seemed to have grown another shoe size. They nearly required the use of a shoehorn to get them into any trainers, but once in, they felt at home.

Even though I managed a couple of hours sleep, it was still broken sleep, as I spent most of the time thinking how I could possibly continue the next day. The thought of another 16 to 18-hour stint filled me with dread. The answer came to me when I was halfway down my wicked-strength glass of black coffee. I should split the day into two halves. Move from three in the morning to midday, take a two-hour break which would hopefully include an hour's sleep, then venture back out for another seven hours graft. My understanding from the first three days was that I managed to progress productively for the first eight to ten hours of the day before slowly falling off the wagon. This resulted in me dragging two stumps along the ground for the penultimate couple of hours of each day. It would drive me to become a foul, aggravated and tormented bear, carrying a ridiculous amount of pain. Therefore, stopping for a break and a nap in the middle of the day before the real discomfort overpowered me, would hopefully allow me to maintain a respectable pace further into the evening, before hitting the hurt locker.

This new approach, along with Melvin making a positive appearance towards the end of the day, contributed to a more productive and slightly less painful day with, thankfully, no repeat of the foot trauma I had felt the day before.

It was also on day four I realised that the diet I had supplied for the challenge wasn't working. The quantity of sugary and fast carb food in my lunch box each day was starting to make me sick, lethargic and loose when going to the toilet. I wasn't used to it; my tongue was already swollen and bumpy, which felt worse from the acidity of the sugar, and my inner lips started to develop spots and sores. So I referred back to my usual diet, which is higher in proteins and fats; this included cooked meats, cheeses, and porridge with nuts and seeds. I kept a few items of the sugary delights for snacks, along with the continued use of the freeze-dried meals. It wasn't long before my tongue started deflating and the soreness in my mouth eased; energy levels became more consistent and my visits to the toilet more regular.

Both these lessons were invaluably important when planning and preparing for the real thing next year in the Arctic.

I did have a nice surprise in the afternoon, which was the company of my mother-in-law. She joined me for a mile or so which lifted my spirits. The pandemic had made her nervous about venturing out, so she only came out when absolutely necessary. I felt honoured that she came to find me, which was multiplied when she handed me a bag full of home-made flapjacks. It was only minutes later I was enjoying picking the remains of them from between my teeth.

Day 5, 57 miles

Another big day, performed in the same manner, referring to a game of two halves. By the end of my five day working week, I had covered 289 miles, with the resulting effect on my body being worrying signs of deterioration. Every part of me was either hurting, bleeding, leaking puss, swollen, chaffed, or fused in one position.

The big deal of the day was being joined by one of my clients, and now friend, Frank. It was Frank's fiftieth birthday, and he was insistent on spending the first few hours of his day accompanying me in my antics. This wasn't a purely unselfish act; this was also to mark a new life direction for him.

Frank first came to me approximately a year earlier with a catalogue of health issues. He was three stone or twenty kilograms overweight, pre-diabetic, suffered bouts of depression and addicted to alcohol, cannabis and cigarettes. He came to me frightened about his future and worried that these addictions were about to have a negative effect on his marriage, including the possibility of putting a wall between him and his son. He decided that walking through my front door and asking for help a year ago was to be his first move. Nine months later, after spending many hours with myself and Mikey, for guidance, balance, positivity and support, the cannabis has gone; alcohol is down to 10% of his usual consumption and he has all but eradicated the cigarettes. Depression has lifted, and he has lost 16 kilograms, with the biggest positive from his hard work being a better home life and the ability to build a better relationship with his wife and son. However, I'm not saying it was a fairy-tale ending. He is constantly fighting demons and revisiting old battlegrounds, day after day, and he will for a long time to come, but his future is looking massively improved from what it once was.

The 18 miles he covered with me that morning was him saying a big thank you to me but, more importantly, to show me he is currently in control and ready to start his fifties with a brighter outlook and a new passion for life.

The morning didn't go quite as we had been planning during the weeks building up to it. We were to have an exciting chat about both our futures, share a coffee or two, and finish with a big breakfast to celebrate his big day. But what actually developed was a game of cat and mouse. We understood early on in the morning that enjoying each other's company wasn't going to work. This was day five for me. I was already well over 200 miles into my week and still trying to survive on three hours of sleep a day. I wasn't in too much of a chatty mood, even though I was trying my hardest to maintain a conversation, and I had two speeds, walking and slowly jogging. Frank's comfortable walking speed was in the middle of my two. This made for an awkward yo-yoing effect as we tried to maintain the other's velocity.

On passing my club I mentioned to Frank that I needed the toilet, to which he replied he would continue travelling along my usual loop around Lutterworth. We decided that I should try to catch him with my intermittent speeds of walking and jogging. An hour later I eventually did, and it was just before we made it back to the club to finish another four-and-a-half-mile loop. This game continued for four hours and four laps, as I always found an excuse to nip into the club for either the toilet or something to eat. Although this wasn't what was on the cards at the beginning of the morning, we both received what we required from the morning's activities. I lost four hours whilst covering a further 18 miles, and Frank managed to start his sixth decade in the way he wanted to - healthy, active and feeling positive.

After Frank went home to celebrate the rest of his big day, I began to fall with each step. The day continued moving at an awfully slow minute at a time. I felt every step, every stumble, every gust of wind and every inch that I covered that afternoon. I went to war with myself, refusing to accept defeat, refusing to allow the pain to influence my performance. I had to finish this on Sunday; I couldn't take this into an eighth day. I had to maintain a level of progress, and it was killing me. My feet were once again in agony. The only way I could continue taking step after step was to get angry. I built a wall to disconnect as much as possible of my sensory awareness of the outside world and disappeared into a solitary existence. Earphones went on, my cap was pulled down just shy of covering my eyes, and a bandana covered my mouth and nose. My hands went into my pockets and I switched everything and everyone off. I do feel guilty about the fact I was ignoring a few friends who came out to walk with me that afternoon, but they understood my situation and gossiped between themselves.

Finishing the day, and being greeted with Teri's comfort and support, I was desperate to cry but refused to show my emotions until the job was done.

Day 6, 54 miles

With 94 miles left, and the need to finish in daylight on the seventh day, I had to accumulate around the mid-fifties in miles again.

Gyula joined me and was a fantastic distraction during the few hours of the early morning darkness, enabling me to download all the stories of the week I had experienced so far. I would even go as far as saying that I didn't feel too much discomfort whilst we chatted away, knocking back a coffee and munching on some nibbles I had stored in the backpack; but it did hit me like a brick wall when he returned home, and I was left to fight my ever-increasing manipulated and malfunctioning body alone. Sticking to my revised plan, I managed to drag myself home at midday so that Teri could work some magic on my feet, and I was lucky enough to grab 40 winks.

One hour later I returned to my legs, and left the house looking for another 20 miles before I was allowed to return for a further break and prepare for round three. I knew the usual two outings wouldn't be sufficient today, especially if I was to pass the chequered flag the next day. During round two I was once again joined by Mikey for a couple of hours. He noticed I was in the worst condition he had ever seen me in, but he managed to lift my spirits as always, like the trooper he is.

Returning home for the second time late in the afternoon, I managed 20 minutes sleep and something warm to eat. I was sat like a zombie on the second step of the stairs, staring at the grain in the woodwork, knowing a round three was needed but petrified of what was on the other side of the door. As I stood up and took a step towards the door, I felt a level of fear as if I would never see my family again if I left. I knew deep down this third stint was never going to go away until I faced it; it had to be done, there was no alternate conclusion, there was no get out clause. It was either do or don't. Now wasn't the time to waiver, so I took another step towards the door, and then another. Just another 10 or 11 miles, that's all I needed.

Halfway down the drive, I glanced back at Teri as she was witnessing her husband visually a foot shorter, 20 years older, limping through both legs, barely able to talk, eyelids swollen so much there was no visible eye left and both leaking, and grasping onto walking poles to prevent him from falling over. I felt her pain as much as I felt mine. I tried to smile to reassure her, to which she smiled back with more love in her eyes than I had ever seen.

There was something different about this evening; it felt personal. Within feet of leaving my home, I felt alone; and when I say alone, I mean, I was the only person left, anywhere. Nothing else and nobody else existed. It was just me against me. I felt I was about to truly meet myself without distraction or disturbance. I felt a warmth, a passion, a resolve building up from inside. I noticed that my senses became acutely tuned to my existence and presence within the world around me; I could see in the dark, sight became more of an intuition. I could smell the earth and the remnant of a perfume from someone who must have passed a few minutes earlier. I could hear the trees creaking, horses chewing hay from across the road and stones crunching under my feet, like an orchestral performance. I felt no pain; the limping changed to a stride as if I were the actor Kevin Spacey at the end of the film 'The Usual Suspects'. I had no need for the walking poles anymore as my speed started increasing past an enthusiastic march on its way to becoming a jog. At this precise moment, Sylvia and Steve appeared in front of me requiring some night-time filming for the documentary. Instantly panicking, I insisted I needed to be on my own - I was about to meet myself. Saying they understood, Sylvia mentioned she would keep her distance, and Steve continued by saying that I wouldn't even notice his presence. I repeated desperately, I needed to be on my own, can you please leave Lutterworth, this is my time. Out of the whole 383 miles of this challenge, these next 10 were mine and mine alone. I NEEDED TO FEEL ALONE. With that, they disappeared, and I continued to fall into my euphoria. It was bliss. I began to cry, but not with despair, pain or discomfort, but because of the overwhelming feeling of joy, compassion and contentment. It was beautiful. I started running, and not the shuffling jog I had been doing the last couple of days. I was running and continued to run for a few miles whilst tears were cascading down my checks, and a grin was invading my inflamed face.

I messaged Teri to join me for the last two miles of the evening so I could share this experience with her, hoping I could lift her as much as I had been lifted, but my words at the time were lost, and my ability to put a sentence together deserted me.

Those two hours will always stay with me, guiding me, giving me strength and hope, whenever desperate times returned, allowing me to keep my head, remain calm, be in control and feel content.

Chapter 15
Day 7 - Time to Go Home

Forty miles left of the 383 miles of the virtual 6633 Arctic Ultra. It's day number seven, and the chequered flag is in sight.

The awakening from the night before, if I can call it that, left an impression so big that the ripples were still being felt. I went straight to sleep and stayed asleep for a full four hours, waking up to a body that although couldn't move and was in obvious torture, had accepted its position and environment, leaving a content and understanding outlook on the day's necessities. Making my way up to my feet, dragging my limbs into clothes, using the facilities, necking a couple of black coffees and a bowl of porridge, I exited the building at two in the morning with a new focus, ambition and direction. There was no apprehension in leaving for another day of torture this time. All pain, tiredness and discomfort were simply accepted as an inevitable hormonal response, and this hormonal response was just the conclusion of the situation I had placed myself in. The key words in that sentence being, 'I had placed myself in'. It was my choice to be right there, right then and in that condition. It was my decision and my decision alone. I had remembered I wanted it; I wanted to know what it felt like to be so broken; I wanted to know what my limits were and what was on the other side, and how would I react to it, and what I would become as a result. Understanding this made the issues simply disappear, becoming irrelevant.

I spent an hour on my own in the darkness of that Sunday morning, feeling gifted that I was about to feel something so accomplishing and satisfying. I was on my own, in the middle of the night, in my hometown surrounded by ten thousand people, all sleeping in their beds, and hopefully dreaming about something or someone special to them. My hometown sits in the south of my local city populated by a further one million people, which is placed in the middle of my country where nearly 70 million other people live, and I can guarantee that I was alone in this quest. I was the only soul walking the streets at two in the morning with such a beaten and dysfunctional body, but with a mind that was so grateful, fulfilled and awakened. I should have felt small, helpless and withdrawn, but I had never felt so much life coursing through me.

After the first hour, Mikey joined me for one more early morning adventure; striding through the streets, arming ourselves with fresh crisp oxygen in our lungs and a large coffee in our hands. The sun rose as if it was just doing it to please us and to let us see the town we now owned. Without us there to witness the occasion it would have just been like any other day, but of course, this wasn't any other day. This was 'the' day, my day. It was time to bring it home, and the sun just wanted to do its bit to show support.

My euphoria continued after Mikey returned to his Sunday morning family breakfast. I can't remember much about the remainder of the morning, apart from managing 21 miles by counting my steps to ten and then repeating the process, again and again and again, until I couldn't move anymore, then retiring for a rest, some food and some foot care.

I headed out for another 12 miles around the local industrial park. It was in this industrial park that I had crossed off a large percentage of my mileage throughout this week and many training days. As far as industrial estates go, it's incredibly quiet, full of trees, shrubs and green land, and is also large enough to be the biggest in Europe. I spent the whole of the 12 miles without passing anyone else. I had the six-mile circuit all to myself, allowing me to efficiently switch to a meditative state. The next three hours disappeared without me being too present. I marched on, staring at the rhythm of my arms, listening to the padding of my feet, standing as tall as possible, and breathing shallowly in and out through my nose. All was perfect until reality struck me round the side of my head like a tossed brick when the pain flooded over me from my toes to my fingertips, nearly sending me to my knees. Luckily, I was heading home to meet Teri for the last 7-miles. Teri started this challenge with me six and a half days earlier, and I was desperate to have her with me as I finished. As I cruised past our home, she was outside waiting. I grabbed her hand without breaking my stride and continued marching. Holding hands is normal practice for us, but on this occasion, it felt more unifying than normal; and besides, I think it was stopping me falling over. I wish our town was a bit bigger so that I didn't have to pass our home one more time before heading to the club and across the line. I do hate retracing my steps when running or walking; I much prefer single loops. But as we passed our home one last time, both our daughters joined in on the ultimate lap and onwards to the finish line.

Three miles to go. It may as well have been 30 miles or even 300 miles; it was a lifetime away. Every second felt like a minute and every minute felt like an hour. I have never known time to stand so still before. Fifteen minutes later another mile clicked by. I intermittently started jogging. It was the same speed as my walking pace but felt quicker and a little more comfortable to be landing on my feet in a different position. Another 15 minutes passed and another mile. I started running. With one mile left, I could smell the finish line. I was visualising crossing the line with so much potency that it was difficult to separate it from reality. The closer I got, the faster I ran; even the girls and Teri struggled to keep up in the last few hundred metres. I had to prevent myself from coming into view of the cheering supporters and waiting for them to catch up so we could all come in together.

Turning the last corner into the parking area of the club with my world in tow, the noise erupted. There was a barrage of cheering, whistling and clapping from all the supporters, some I knew and some I didn't. Counting the last 10 steps towards the yellow and black speed bump, which I used as the start and finish line, I gave the most growling, throat-tearing shout of excitement I could muster, stepped over the twelve-foot-long stripped bump and went to the floor to meet the tarmac with my forehead. Lying face down, breathing heavily, I could see the dust in the crevasses beneath my mouth being blown away. The cheering, chanting and appreciation continued on and on for as long as I stayed on the ground. I soaked up every single decibel of it. I was swimming in my own glory with satisfied contentment that I had no more work to do today. The job was done.

Rising to my knees, I eyed a few faces that had seen me through the week and was desperate to let them know my appreciation; but first, I needed a hug from my wife who must have been through her own roller coaster. She looked as tired as me, but with the biggest, proudest, beaming smile on her face. As we made eye contact, she came towards me. I tried to meet her height but could only manage to give her hips a big hug. I managed to high five, fist bump, hug or shake hands with everyone before reaching Mikey, and that was when the tears tried to squeeze past my swollen eyelids. I could see myself through his eyes, and could feel the pride he felt without him moving a muscle or saying a word.

Moments later I was sitting outside the club with a bucket of ice in front of me, which was there waiting to accept my feet and start the healing process. Everyone was slowly gathering around me, asking questions and listening to my responses, they were feeling very much part of my energy. That was, until I took my socks off to put my feet into the ice. I've never heard so many people in unison go "Oooh, that's nasty", and back away whilst looking at sky. The scenario continued to repeat in my head for days after, as I privately chuckled.

Returning home, I noticed the smallest of things giving me pleasure. The extra-long shower; fresh clothes; my daughter talking to me about a programme she had been watching; a pillow; eating with my family. Sleep was an issue for days afterwards. I would only sleep sporadically for an hour at a time, an hour on the sofa midday, an hour on the floor in the afternoon, and an hour in bed in the middle of the night. Sometimes it was through pain, sometimes shivering, sometimes sweats, and other times I would simply just wake up in a panic feeling I was late for something. During the event I accumulated no more than twenty hours sleep, and I can't say it was much more than that throughout the week after, either. I also didn't stop eating for a couple of weeks. I only lost one kilogram during the week, but I lost a further three and a half the week after as my stress levels slowly returned to normal, and my body began repairing.

It wasn't just me, either. It affected the whole family, especially Teri. For a couple of weeks, she was worried about her lack of energy, inability to get out of bed in the morning, and her emotionless response to life. She had shared every step, every blister, every tear and every discomfort though our incredible week. She deserves the accolade as much as I did.

Chapter 16
Last Thoughts

So, as I sat on my sofa, two weeks after I walked through my front door from completing 383 miles in six days and fifteen hours, finishing what was, undoubtedly, the hardest challenge I have ever set myself, I pondered...why? Why did I feel it so necessary to push myself to such levels of pain and discomfort?

This is usually around the time most ultra-athletes start thinking, what's next? It's around the time the emptiness fills the days that were once filled with training, planning and researching. As I sat there, I didn't need the 'what next' question answered. I already knew what was next. I knew what my plans were, for at least the next 12 months, anyway. My question was, why? Why do I need to do more? Why is it that, within days of completing such a mammoth challenge, do I go straight back to the search engines for the next adventure; the adventures that create so much stress and apprehension, not just for me, but for my family and friends? I have to admit, I'm sometimes not the best to live around when building up to an event. I'm grumpy, agitated and snappy, and, as I get closer to race day, I can spend a lot of my time apologising for my directness and assertiveness.

I had just experienced over six days of pure torture, blisters on blisters, swelling in every joint from the ankles to the wrists, stomach cramps, inflamed tongue and mouth, mentally destroyed to the point that counting to ten was a chore, experiencing sleep demons from three hours sleep a night, dehydration and malnutrition, and ultimately finding my euphoric moment. Why do I want to do it all again? Why does the need for more outweigh the need to recover and hang up the running shoes?

It's the journey! It's the journey that gives us life and not just an existence; it's the journey that encourages excitement, anticipation and character. It's the journey that feeds growth, strength, knowledge, and evolution; it's the journey that makes us human. Without a journey, without the personal gain and development you receive from a journey, all you have left is instant gratification, one of the biggest enemies of the modern world. Instant gratification is a dangerous and unfulfilling disease, and it has friends; they are called depression and anxiety. This duo of destruction is supposedly affecting fifty percent of the first world's population. It's a pandemic never seen before in humankind.

By receiving everything when it's wanted, watching a whole box set as soon as it's released, buying something without earning it first, or achieving a goal without the need to work for it, takes away the part of the process that we call 'life'. This leaves a massive hole; an unknown and unsatisfactory space that needs filling. How many times have you heard someone mention how empty they feel, and how much they are longing for something to happen? The emptiness that is felt when the journey is taken away is where depression, anxiety and dissatisfaction can grow and prosper.

Generally speaking, I would say that we in the first world live a relatively comfortable lifestyle, where the only challenges we face are passing exams or tests, applying for jobs or moving to a new house, etc. We force ourselves into a gym a couple of times a week to take away the guilt and consequence of indulgence. We get up in the morning to spend a few hours a day in a job we don't particularly like, to earn enough money to pay for the mortgage that covers the purchase of our wonderfully comfortable, well-heated castles, full of luxuries and comforts; and, additionally, to pay for our mobile phones, Netflix, alcohol and meals in the local restaurant. We get trapped in this well-groomed existence, trying to find something to fill the gap where the journey once lived. I'm not judging anyone, I do it too, which is the exact reason I need another event, another challenge; something I must work towards in order to be successful. I need something I could fail at if I'm not prepared; something that will beat me to a pulp while facing it head-on in order to build resilience; something that will make me learn and grow. I'm missing journeys in my life. My genes miss the journeys they experienced day after day, which encouraged evolution and adaptation, journeys that were so prevalent throughout my ancestral history, teaching me lessons so that I might stay alive. From the dawn of humanity until very recently, life itself was the journey; a challenge to survive, a challenge to feed, and a challenge to keep warm. To find and secure these basic needs for ourselves and our loved ones *was* the journey. As mentioned, we don't have the same journey or challenges anymore; we just have the victory, the purchase, the glory - the instant gratification - the big hole.

Let's look at the word 'journey'. What signifies a journey? A journey could be something that will take you from point A to point B. This could be leaving your home and arriving at your place of work. It could be deciding to work towards owning the new BMW 3 series (point A) and actually driving it onto the driveway (point B). It could be picking a holiday destination in January (point A) and lying on the beach six months later (point B).

Maybe it could be picking the right courses to become an engineer (A) and walking into your new position as an apprentice engineer at the local automotive plant (B). There are even bigger journeys, like the moment you chose to have a child and then supporting your child as they, 25 years later, give birth to your grandchild.

The need for a journey is so powerful that, without it, the victory is insignificant. There have been nearly 5000 people who have reached the top of Mount Everest. If it were possible to catch a helicopter to the top of this infamous creation, how many of those 5000 adventurers would have chosen to be dropped at the top only to be then taken back down 30 minutes later after admiring the view with a cup of coffee. I would put my money on there not being a single one of them; not even one would have chosen the easier instantly gratifying route. It wasn't about standing on the top. It was about the 18 months of training, preparing and researching. It's about the journey, effort, understanding and growth it took for them to earn the right to be able to stand there. Similarly, saving for three years, by grinding out hour after hour of overtime so you can walk into the showroom with your hard-earned money in your hand and purchase that BMW 3 series instead of getting a three-year loan, would make owning the BMW more sweet, more satisfying and more rewarding. You would feel a greater sense of appreciation and achievement every time you sat in the driver's seat, cleaned and polished it or filled it with fuel. You would remember the journey, the effort, the sweat and tears it took to acquire it.

Why is it that, passing your school, college or university exams, or even passing your driving test, are all still recognised as the most fulfilling achievements you will feel as a young adult? This is because you still have to go through the journey. You still have to go through months, if not years, of studying and worrying before the glory is felt. There is no instant gratification. If you don't work hard, you fail. If you put the hours in, work hard, go through discomfort, you will be successful, and that success is more greatly felt because of the effort needed to

210

stand on the pride pedestal and say, I did that. The greater the effort, the greater the journey; the greater the journey, the higher the pedestal.

Every journey comes with an element of risk, and it's this risk that creates life. Without risk there is no glory; without glory there is no sense of achievement; without the sense of achievement there is no growth, adaptation or evolution. After all, achievement is the other side of the coin of failure, and we already know how important that is.

We need risk in our life; it keeps us on our toes. It makes the heart beat stronger, wakes us in the morning, builds excitement and anticipation and becomes addictive; the bigger the risk, the bigger the life development. If we weren't willing to take risks, we would never buy a house or even leave the house, or go to university, change jobs, talk to anyone new, go on holiday, buy a car, fall in love or become a parent.

Risk has always been part of our future, continually sitting on our shoulders as we swung through the trees, then stumbled around on two legs, then dwelled in caves, developed fire, built mud huts and hunted animals: the bigger the risk, the greater the reward and the further the advancement, creating better odds for survival. All risks need to be calculated. Some people are happier taking greater risks than others, but to move forward in life, risks have to be taken.

Ancestral risks could range from, whether to go out hunting and gathering on a stormy day, to, is it worth challenging that mammoth for food or shall I settle for the rodent? Not going out on a stormy day could mean another day starving, but conversely, going out could mean illness or injury. We would need to calculate the risk. Taking down a mammoth could mean food for the entire village until bellies are full for a week, increasing the chances of surviving the harsh winter, but it could also mean death for you and possible death of your family because their hunter had been killed: whereas killing the rodent was safer but wouldn't supply the calories needed to keep warm through the night. We would need to calculate the risk. In order to have made it to a ripe old age as a cave dweller, you would need to have made countless risk assessments, each time becoming more experienced, better equipped and more calculated with your judgments. This newly-learnt judgment of hazardous situations, when passed down to children, would give them a better chance of surviving. The more risks taken, and the better judgement calls calculated from the ever-increasing risk-taking would mean a better chance of surviving.

Unfortunately, in modern times we have eliminated as much as possible the need to take risks. Not only are we growing into a culture that is risk-averse, but we fall drastically when a small risk goes wrong: for example, giving your all in a job interview, only to fail; putting yourself out on a ledge by asking out the heartthrob next door, only to be turned down; or even buying yourself a new gift without consulting your partner, only to be told we really can't afford it and you'll have to take it back. These are small risks and should be easily rolled off the back if they go wrong. But they don't; these small bumps in the road are knocking some people into submission, and this submission is leading to high levels of stress and anxiety.

Further up the risk mountain are medium size risks: where do I invest my money; should we buy or rent a property; where should we live, and should I go to the Arctic to challenge myself in a possibly harmful and life-threatening environment?

Then come the life-changing risks: should I agree to spend the rest of my life with this person; should we have children, or should we emigrate?

These are all risks that most of us will have to deal with at some point during our lives, from the small everyday risks to the large life changing risks. The problem, as I see it, is the wrapped-in-cotton-wool culture, we have subconsciously created. It might make our day-to-day life easy and comfortable, but it's taken away the small risks we need in order to experience and learn from, in order to build the resilience we need to bounce back from them, thus creating a new generation of young adults that lack the developmental skills and knowledge required to grow, learn, adapt and develop.

Social media hasn't helped. It has the ability to make its users feel like they are the centre of the universe. Who in their right mind would take even the smallest of risks if everything they did was scrutinised in front of hundreds and thousands of people? Dangerously, a lot of people live in a world that needs approval from a group of strangers for every single action they take. What they are having for dinner; how far they are running; what they have just bought from the supermarket, and if they have decided to have a pyjama day. So, putting themselves on a pedestal when the world is watching and possibly showing failure, is far too scary and it's stopping people taking risks. Therefore, it's stopping progression, development, character building and passion.

It's very dangerous to believe you are the centre of the universe. That is too much power for one brain to live with. Experiencing a journey, taking a risk and possibly failing, keeps us humble; it reminds us we are only human. It encourages us to live for ourselves and not for the hundreds of unknown viewers on social media that actually don't even care about what you do with your life and what you are eating for dinner.

Living a pretend life in front of a mobile phone, looking for approval from others during your artificial adventures, is safer than having an actual adventure for yourself, because it's scary to do something just for you. We are in a constant state of dependency for this companionship we get from our piece of technology. But safe isn't always the best way. Cars and motorbikes (I love my motorbike) are safer in the garage than on the road, but what fun is that? They are built for excitement and to take you on a journey, but that journey has a certain level of risk to it. Staying locked away in your castle without allowing anyone to emotionally connect with you is safer than taking the gamble and asking out the neighbour for a date, but what a lonely existence that would be. What better way to experience the journey of life than with another person? Exercising in the local gym and running around the track is safer than going to the Arctic and risking drastic failure at a great expense. But where's the fun in that? It isn't a life, it's just an existence. We, as human beings, are built to live, gamble and take risks. We are built to fail, learn and repeat until success is achieved, and then, take another risk, continuing to fail until a new lesson is learnt before we can move forward again. This is what we do. This is how we've become who we are.

So, without the journey and without the risk, what do we have left? A mundane, flat emotionless life full of holes that constantly require filling by the instant gratification that temporarily gives us a break from the emptiness that encourages depression and anxiety: a life lacking self-respect or self-confidence; a life lacking achievement or glory, and a life without progression, development or awareness.

Having self-awareness or, another way of saying it, knowing yourself, is the most important state of mind from which to challenge life. How do you know what sort of person you are - what you are capable of, what you're not capable of, what sort of partner, father, mother, friend, boss or work colleague you are - if you don't know yourself? How can you possibly and honestly contemplate answering any questions about yourself if you haven't pushed yourself to the edge to see what's on the other side: if you haven't tested your character to find its limits, and what happens when those limits are exceeded? If you haven't experienced rejection, failure, disappointment or loss, and then experienced the knowledge, growth and emotional development needed to cope with it, how do you know you have what it takes to continue moving forward?

This is the WHY I asked myself at the very beginning! I need a journey; I need to take risks and I need to find out who I am. By living my life, constantly searching for these, makes me more capable of being the best father, husband, friend, boss, colleague and human I can be. It constantly encourages growth on every level, and it allows me to have a life, not an existence.

One last thought, and it comes in the form of a question to you.

What are you actually capable of? What is your best? Just once, one time in your life, what is your maximum? If you put all your heart and soul into one moment; everything you've failed at, everything you've succeeded at, all your learning, all your passion, all your energy, all your anger and love, frustration and determination; every thought process, every decision you've made. If you gave absolutely everything that makes you, you, just once, what does that look like? Is it something worth looking up to? Is it something that will inspire others? More importantly, is it something that will encourage your children to live their best life? And lastly, would it be something that would make you smile in your last days?

DON'T FAIL...LEARN!

Acknowledgements

My wife and my two daughters; are my world, my strength and my purpose. I thank Teri for always being there, for never holding me back, for always showing as much enthusiasm for my stupid and sometimes strange adventures as I did, and for being my rock, my sanity, my nurse, my best friend and my piece of the jigsaw. Without her the whole picture would be worthless. My ideas, challenges and schemes have occasionally placed us in difficult situations, but she has never questioned or doubted me, always pushing me to live a life without regret. Without Teri, I would still be the same person I was at the beginning of the book.

Becoming a father and taking that responsibility seriously has, and still is, one of the hardest, but most satisfying and rewarding roles I have taken on. My daughters are the reason I get up and push myself every day. Everything I do has an alternative motive, which is to show them how to be a happy, balanced, wise and successful people, with the ability, drive and love to fight for everything they deserve. Now that they are both young adults, they are showing signs that they have listened, watched and absorbed my lessons. I would like to thank them for that: it's a lot easier to be a teacher when you feel your words are being processed. I am extremely proud and incredibly grateful to be part of their worlds.

Throughout the years I have spent with Teri, we have always had the unwavering support, guidance and backing from Vera, Teri's mother. On many occasions she would believe we were making wrong decisions, following the wrong path, or getting ourselves into trouble, but would still support us in whatever way she could, knowing we could either fail or succeed, but ultimately grow. So, thank you.

Vera was also one of my editors for the book, along with two great friends, Emma and Rosie. I am beyond grateful for their sacrificed time in helping me at the drop of a hat. Their advice, suggestions and attention to detail has helped me create a book I am enormously proud of and excited about. Thank you.

The three biggest people in my life, that prove that family isn't necessary blood-related are Mikey, Gyula and Sylvia: the three pillars that hold me together. Mikey for his ability to know exactly what I need, even if I don't know myself. His spiritual calmness and his energy are grounding, and stops me from becoming distracted by the impurities in life and losing focus. Gyula for his unrelenting, unwavering and unquestioning friendship; his support, trust and devotion to a friendship that, to be honest, I didn't always deserve. Sylvia for her faith and trust in my ambitions and capabilities. In the relatively short period of time we have been part of each other's worlds, she has looked out for me, continuing to make sure I dot the 'I's and cross the 'T's. She has gone way beyond any expectations of a work colleague, or even a friend. Sylvia, along with Mikey and Gyula, are family, and I look forward to seeing what adventures we can share together in the future.

I would also like to take this opportunity to give a big shout out to Karl. He was such a massive influence at the beginning of my transition. We don't see each other as much as we should, but he will always be very important to me. The week we spent in Chamonix will also be one of my best memories.

I would like to say a massive thank you to Steve and Kane for their time spent making my documentaries which have supported this book. They both went beyond their promises, making me look better than I thought possible.

Another great friend is Albert who gave me many hours of his time cracking my body back into shape, and manipulating my muscles enough so they could continue to perform day after day.

Lastly, SB Health and Fitness. Firstly, for the financial support in covering most of the expenses during this year, and the year I am about to experience, ending with participating in the 6633 Arctic Ultra. Secondly, and most importantly, I want to thank the community within the club. I tip my hat to every one of them. We haven't had the best opportunity to develop as a club or a community because of the short amount of time we were open before Covid-19 closed us down, but the support, energy, devotion and loyalty has exceeded anything I could have expected. With the world now opening again, I am extremely excited to see what we are capable of and what adventures the years to come will give us.